GARDNER'S
guide to
Animation Scriptwriting
The Writer's Road Map

by Marilyn Webber

GGC Inc./*Publishing*

Fairfax, Virginia

Art Director: Nic Banks
Editor: Bonney Ford
Assistant to the Editor: Wendell Howard
Cover Illustration: Mitsuaki Yajima
Cover Design: Nic Banks
Publisher: G. Gardner, Ph.D.

Editorial inquiries concerning this book should be addressed to the editor at GGC, Inc, 4602 John Hancock Ct. 302, Annandale, VA 22003

This publication is designed to provide accurate and authoritative information in regard to the subject matter covered. It is sold with the understanding that the publisher is not engaged in rendering professional services. If professional advice or other expert assistance is required, the services of a competent professional person should be sought.

"Gardner's Guide" is a trademark of GGC, Inc.

Library of Congress Cataloging-in-Publication Data
Webber, Marilyn.

Gardner's Guide to Animation Scriptwriting: The Writer's Road Map/ Marilyn Webber.
p. cm.
Includes bibliographical references and index.
ISBN 0-9661075-9-4 (pbk)
    1. Script Writing – Vocational guidance. 2. Writing Animation – Vocational guide.
3. Writing Guide – How-to. 4. Script Writing – Hand book, reference.

Library of Congress Control Number: 00-134372

Printed in Canada

The most wasted of all days is that in which we have not laughed.
— Sebastien R.N.Chamfort, *Maximes et pensees.*

This book is dedicated to every writer who will struggle and who has struggled to make people laugh.

Table of Contents

Acknowledgments

I could not begin this book without acknowledging Linda Steiner at Warner Bros. who offered me my first official writing assignment in animation, and to whom I am privileged to call my friend. I would also like to thank Joe Ruby and Ken Spears at Ruby/Spears Productions for treating me like one of the family during each and every freelance assignment. I truly enjoyed plotting out stories with such a talented story teller. Thank you, Joe.

In addition, thanks to my publisher, Garth Gardner, whose enthusiasm and expertise has guided me in the writing process of this book. I want to extend my gratitude to Tina San Lucas and DIC Entertainment as well for allowing me to include one of my scripts that I wrote for their cartoon series, What-A-Mess, in this book.

To all my teachers, both past and future, I send my heartfelt gratitude for making my journey of learning a fascinating one. To all my students, both past and future, I also wish to say, "Thank you," for compelling me to continue stretching as both a writer and a teacher.

Last, but certainly not least, to every animation writer and storyboard artist, whose work has inspired my passion for cartoon writing, and whose names are too numerous to list here, bless you. To each of you, I owe the most.

— Marilyn Webber

About the Author

Marilyn Webber has worked as a professional writer in Los Angeles for the past eight years. Earning her M.F.A. at *The American Film Institute*, her work has garnered nominations for both an ACADEMY AWARD and a HUMANITAS. In addition, her work has won an *NAACP Award*, an *NEA Award:* For The Advancement of Learning in Broadcasting, an *American Association Library Award:* For Most Notable Children's Video, and winner of *The Indiana Film Festival.*

Miss Webber began her career in children's programming, writing Saturday morning cartoons and animation teleplays until writing one hour action/adventure and dramas for both day time and prime time television. During this period, her romantic comedy screenplay, *How To Kill Howie,* won Best Screenplay at the Texas Film Festival, while her science fiction script, *The Lawless Legion,* her action script, *Mouth of the Cat,* her drama, *A Place Called Harmony,* and television spec for *NYPD Blue: Suffer the Little Children,* all placed as Semi-finalists in The Writer's Foundation America's Best Contest.

She has freelanced for networks such as ABC and CBS, and for studios such as Universal and Disney. Her screenplays have been optioned by numerous producers including those at Hearst Entertainment, Saban Entertainment, and Paramount Pictures. Currently, her feature film, "Murder Seen" is being produced by Saban Entertainment to be released soon.

Miss Webber has taught creative writing extension courses through Johns Hopkins University IAAY program, as well as giving independent seminars on screenwriting and writing for animation. Occasionally, she consults as script analyst. A member of the Writer's Guild of America, she has also been a judge for the Cable Ace Awards in the category of dramatic writing.

Currently, she has completed a historical novel, and is developing it as a mini-series. She continues to freelance for television, and is pursuing producing and directing her first feature film. She is the author of *Gardner's Guide to Screenwriting: The Writer's Road Map.*

Preface

Animation Scriptwriting: The Writer's Road Map allows you to work at your own pace, although I recommend not letting too much time pass between chapters unless specified to do so. If your schedule prohibits you from working on the exercises weekly, then it's a good idea to reread previous chapters before continuing forward.

It's important not to skip any of the exercises in your enthusiasm to start writing your first animated script. The exercises are building blocks, and each one is designed to help you identify the story elements in other cartoons, which will strengthen the development of your own script.

In the beginning chapters, the exercises ask you to view numerous cartoons. Be sure to choose cartoons you don't mind watching over and over because you'll need to review these episodes throughout the book.

As you study other cartoon series, you'll also be starting your own scripts. This book navigates you through the writing process each step of the way, working in sections, until you cross the finish line and have two animated teleplays in front of you.

Animation writing is a process. It takes perseverance, dedication, hard work, and knowledge of the animation process to become a successful cartoon writer. *Gardner's Guide to Animation Scriptwriting: The Writer's Road Map* will give you the knowledge needed to create and pitch your ideas as well as how to execute them into a humorous script. The rest is up to you. So get ready, get set, go!

Introduction

This book is for writers who want to expand their writing venues and venture into animation writing. It is also for the beginning writer. If you have a passion for writing, and never truly grew up, that is, you still watch cartoons (thank goodness for prime-time animation shows) then why not combine the two? Animation writing is fun, and can be a great source of income (not to mention, you'll actually have an excuse to watch cartoons – you're researching!).

As a writer, animation writing is often more accessible to break into than the domain of television or film. You can often get your sample animation scripts read by a story editor without having an agent. Also, there just isn't as much competition in animation writing as there is in TV or film writing. This most likely is due to the fact that animation writing isn't protected by the Writer's Guild of America, and therefore, a writer receives no residuals from the episodes he or she writes (there are prime-time exceptions).

Even so, writing for animation can still be a gold mine for a writer, especially for those of you who are just starting your writing careers. With the existence of cable networks such as Warner Brothers, Nickelodeon, and FOX, along with the major networks' Saturday morning cartoons, animation writers are more sought after now than ever before. (If you noticed I didn't include The Cartoon Network above, that's because generally it uses animators to both write and animate their series.)

Animation Scriptwriting: The Writer's Road Map will show, through simple analogy, the basics of writing for animation. It will offer distinctions between animation and live-action scripts, examine cartoon genres, and cover the basic animation structures: 22 minute, 11 minute and 7 minute scripts. In addition, it explains character types, studies scene construction, teaches dialogue devices and lists mechanisms of humor used in animation writing.

It does not include writing for animated features, although many of the issues discussed here will apply to feature animation. (For those of you wanting to write a feature animated script, use the rules of this book combined with the structure of the feature script in *Screenwriting: The Writer's Road Map*.)

In animation writing, you'll find there are do's and don'ts. Likewise, there are certain broadcasting guidelines you must know. *Animation Scriptwriting: The Writer's Road Map* will also decipher terms inherent to the process of animation writing: terms such as springboard, premise, treatment, and beat outline. The last chapter describes how to get your scripts read by story editors, and pitch your newly written springboards.

For those of you who have an animated series idea and want to develop it into a series and a script, this book will reveal how. For those of you who just want to write for existing cartoon series, then this book will guide you in creating sample scripts you can use as "calling cards." Through various exercises, you will develop springboards and complete two animated teleplays by the end of the book.

Regardless of what you seek to glean from the *Animation Scriptwriting: The Writer's Road Map*, this book will speed you onto the road of animation writing in an easy manner. It is a culmination of everything I have learned while writing for animation during the ten years of my professional career. It also includes information collected from executives, story editors, and animators along the way, both in the United States and abroad.

So, if you love cartoons and you love to write, start reading. By the time you finish Chapter One, you'll be on your way to a fun and exciting career. As you'll soon discover, having a "Peter Pan" syndrome can actually pay off – at least in the world of animation writing.

Chapter One
Animation: An Overview

Animation v. Live-Action

So just how does animation differ from live-action? Well, this is where our highway divides because in live-action, the rules of the universe apply, that is, there are laws of physics. If a truck smashes into you at eighty mph, you can't "unflatten" yourself, erase the tread marks, and be on your merry way – you're dead!

Put another way, when a bomb goes off in live-action, and the hero is holding it, we've just witnessed a tragedy. He can't wipe off his ashen face or put his limbs back together. As an audience, we know he's dead and he's not coming back to life (okay, maybe if he's Freddy Kruger, he is, but that's a horror genre where the laws of physics don't always apply).

A devastating event in live-action is what's funny in the cartoon world. When an animated character runs off a cliff, falls two hundred feet and is flattened by a boulder, we laugh. Why, you ask? Is it because as human beings we are sick and twisted? No. (Well, maybe just a little.) We laugh because we know cartoon characters don't die – they're animated! This doesn't mean they can't react to the "pain;" it just means we know their pain isn't real. A cartoon character can handle any catastrophe, return to his/ her normal self, and continue happily (or grumpily) on his/ her animated way.

In an animated universe, the laws of physics no longer apply; characters can be squashed flat like a bug, rolled up into a ball, stretched like taffy, or break into a million pieces and put themselves back together again. They can perform physical acts, known as cartoon physical feats, that live-action characters cannot. For example, a cartoon character can extend his arm ten feet from his body, but a human being can't. We can't flap our arms and fly or be bounced around like a ball or spin our feet like wheels while hanging in mid-air. None of these things can happen in live-action films (and we're talking about the genres which don't suspend the laws of physics) but in cartoons, they can and must happen. We love to watch animated film precisely because it does not conform to the laws of our physical world.

Let's look at some examples of cartoon physical feats found in the episodes below:

In *Ape Is Enough* (*Johnny Bravo*), Pop's eyes literally become dollar signs (a classic cartoon feat). In *Johnny and the Beanstalk*, the Giant uses Johnny as a badminton ball.

In *Dee Dee's Tail* (*Dexter's Laboratory*) two heavy metal slabs smash Dee Dee, then re-open to reveal she's changed into a pony.

In *The Temple of Eliza* (*The Thornberry's*), the native, Donnie, spins around like a tornado as he sets the table.

Cartoon writers and animators rely on defying the laws of physics by using cartoon physical feats to create their humor, and this is what makes animation unique from other writing mediums.

Animation Concepts

If you are developing your own half-hour cartoon series in hopes of selling it to a network, then you need to understand what such executives look for in an "original" cartoon concept. There are three main sources executives work from when developing cartoons for television:

1 Classic Cartoon Characters

2 Marquee Characters

3 Original Concepts

Let's take a further look at these three concepts.

Classic Cartoon Characters

Classic cartoon characters have what network executives call "marquee value." This means they are familiar, and therefore already have a built-in audience. Network and television executives most often develop series from this angle because they don't want to spend hundreds of thousands of dollars just to introduce a new character no one's ever heard of. This is why you'll always see cartoon series such as *The New Adventures Of Winnie The Pooh* and *The Adventures of Jonny Quest* which take classic characters and update them for today's audience.

Likewise, cartoon lineages play an important role because new characters can be created from old characters and given a similar look. In this way, the characters will have a familiarity to the audience because they stem from pre-existing characters that have been around for decades. In the early 1990's, the trend was to take classic characters such as Yogi Bear and the gang, and make them younger. *Yo, Yogi!* turned the bear into a teenager who hung out at the shopping mall with his friends. *A Pup Named Scooby Doo* made Scooby a much younger dog than the original.

One of the best usages of a cartoon lineage is *Tiny Toons*. In a brilliant twist, *Tiny Toons* drew from the *Looney Toon Gang* lineage, making their characters children of such famous and well-loved cartoon classics as Bugs Bunny and Daffy Duck. In doing so, they came up with a very clever and successful cartoon. This is known as taking an old idea, and making it high-concept. High-concept means an idea which can be pitched clearly in a few sentences, and immediately illustrate its marketability. If you want to pitch your own cartoon series, you want to make sure your idea is high-concept because for executives, the bottom line is money. How much revenue will your series generate for them? If they can see mega dollar signs, then your series idea is a go.

Marquee Ideas

These are ideas or concepts which capitalize on the previous success of films, comic books, film stars, video games and comic strips. If you want to create a series from an existing marquee, then you must obtain the option right to do so.

For example, *Ace Ventura Pet Detective* – from the film, *Garfield & Friends* - from the famous cartoon strip, *Sabrina* - from the prime time sitcom and characters created in the *Archie* comic books, and *Madeline* - from a children's book series.

Original concepts

This is the third way cartoons are developed for television, and are the hardest to get off the ground at a network or studio because they require an enormous amount of time, money and energy to introduce, produce, and promote. FOX, MTV, and the Comedy Channel, however, have proven that unknown characters can be extremely profitable, with the enormous triumph of *The Simpsons* and *South Park*. In fact, *The Simpsons* just celebrated their tenth anniversary, making the cartoon series the currently longest running animated sitcom on the air today.

In spite of such successes, executives often prefer to base "original" characters from a toy or game which has a proven market value. For example, *GI Joes* (toy) *Pok'emon* (card game) or *Blasters* (based on educational software programs) have a ready-made audience based on their existing markets.

No matter how you develop your series, keep in mind that cartoons are almost always geared for boys because boys after age six are very cautious about what they watch. Studies show they steer clear of anything remotely girlish. That's why most girl characters in cartoons are tomboyish so as not to scare off the young male audience. The studies have indicated girls, will watch a variety of series because they have a better sense of themselves and are not so gender oriented.

For those of you who wish to develop a series on spec (writing on the speculation that you will sell it) then you will have to construct a cartoon bible for your series.

Note: For those of you who just want to learn how to write a script for a pre-existing series, the following information below will be valuable to you as well.

Cartoon Bibles

All cartoon series have what is known as a cartoon or series bible. The story editors create, usually with notes from executives and producers, the series bible which contains all the details and restrictions of that particular cartoon. Generally, the series bible consists of 30 to 45 pages (plus another 20-25 pages of illustrations) encompassing the following:

1 Title page listing the title of the show and the writers with a series logo.

2 If needed, any myth or legend which explains how this particular cartoon world came into being. (1-3 pages)

> Following, is an excerpt from *C.O.W. Boys Of Moo Mesa* series bible:
>
> "Truth is, nobody can say for sure what happened...In the days of real cowboys,...things were wild, includin' the weather...Best anybody can tell is a (comet buried) itself deep in Moo Mesa... With the shard bein' from outer space and all, well, it...figure(s) that things could get mighty peculiar..."
>
> Gunther-Wahl Productions

3 A summary or overview of what the series is about, including a brief listing of the main characters and villains. (1-3 pages)

Below, is an excerpt from *Tale Spin* series bible:

> "Welcome to a world of wonders. A place where the airplane is king,...men are men, and eagles are nervous...Soar the docksides of Cape Suzette..., swoop over sweltering jungles...Mingle with entrepreneurs..., seedy con men...Prepare...to visit a land where life('s) constantly an escapade. Welcome to *Tale Spin*..."
>
> Disney

4 The settings and location backgrounds, describing each of these. (1-4 written pages plus illustrations of sets and locales)

An excerpt from *Dark Water* series bible:

"The Wraith is the stolen vessel Ren sails on his quest...(It's) a mix of 14th Century technology and...of the ecologically based Merian maritime civilization. The swiftest craft on the seas..., (it) features a dynamic wing-like mainsail that can be detached and used as a...hang glider..."

Written by Sean Roche

5   It also lists all the rules of the series particular "cartooniverse." The cartooniverse is the world where the characters live and breathe. Each cartoon series will have its own specific rules about its own world. (1-4 pages)

Note: We'll take a look at some cartooniverse rules below.

6   A compilation of all characters, describing each and every character, including the villain, and their backstories. The bible also explains each character's relationship to every character on the show. Illustrations of how each of the characters will look and move will also be included. (5-25 written pages depending on the format length: 22, 11 or 7 minutes plus illustrated pages)

Below is an excerpt from *Yo Yogi!* series bible:

> "Like most teenagers, Snagglepuss has three subjects he knows everything about: anything, everything, and himself. Hammy and grandiose, Snag is an overwrought actor whose only training appears to be in bad Shakespeare...His supply of costumes and disguises are limitless...Like most windbags, this mountain lion is chicken."

Hanna-Barbera Productions

7   The set-up of what the show will be about each week. In addition, include half a dozen springboards of sample episodes for the series.

Below is a springboard from *What-A-Mess*:

> "Neither rain, snow or What-A-Mess is going to keep the Mail Carrier from delivering the special package. The young pup is equally determined to keep this crafty "intruder" from his family's home. In a James Bond parody, the Mail Carrier makes

delivering the package a covert operation, causing the pup to don his cape - it's Super What-A-Mess to the rescue."

Note: We will discuss springboards in greater length in Chapter 17.

8 The tone of the show which might include more rules of the cartooniverse, and/or style of dialogue for the show. You can sprinkle a couple of lines of dialogue here for effect - just make sure they're very good lines. (1-2 pages)

Below is an excerpt from *The Addams Family* series bible:

> "…The…macabre humor is…never sick, demented, or gross…The Addams do not eat…bugs or body parts. But…have serve(d) a…breakfast that may…wander around the house…Likewise, (they)…would never throw anyone into their pirana Jacuzzi. But that doesn't keep Fester from…treating himself to an invigorating dip."
>
> Written by Bill Matheny & Lane Raichert

Notice in the above examples, the writers capture the tone of their show in each section of the series bible. Really strut your stuff as a writer in the cartoon bible. If you are developing your own series, this is your sales pitch – make it brilliant!

I promised examples of cartooniverse rules, so how about starting with the most classic:

Wiley E. Coyote schemes in every episode to catch that blasted Road Runner, and poor Wiley is doomed to always fail.

Another cartooniverse rule which is now a classic with teenagers today, can be found in *South Park*. In every episode, little Kenny dies a visually gruesome death, only to return, in the next episode.

In *Cow & Chicken*, we never see the parents except from the waist down. Other adults in the series are shown in their entirety, but not the parents. That means as a writer, you must be careful not to break this rule. You can't write, "Cow's mom smiles at him." If we can't see her face, we can't see her smile. Be mindful of each and every cartooniverse rule of a particular series when writing your sample script.

In one of my favorite cartoons, *Count Duckula*, all the characters in the series are types of bird. If you introduced a character in this series, you would have follow this rule.

In *Rescue Heroes*, the writer must always include a safety tip which is repeated at least once throughout the episode.

Likewise, in *Blasters*, there is always a brief lesson taught, usually one on science. For example, *Sound Advice*, explained how dogs hear differently than humans.

In the first animated series I wrote for, *C.O.W. Boys Of Moo Mesa*, the heroes were cows, who through a cosmic event had been given human traits. They could talk and ride horses just like cowboys. One of the rules of their cartooniverse was that only the animals that were outside (unsheltered) when the cosmic shard went over the Mesa became humanized (that's how they explain humanized cows riding regular horses). Thus, there are other animals in the show who cannot speak or walk upright in the *Moo Mesa* cartooniverse.

In *Garfield & Friends*, Garfield's lips never move when he's talking. In addition, Garfield doesn't have super powers either, so you can't write an episode in which he suddenly flies and leaps tall skyscrapers in a single bound. This isn't part of his cartooniverse.

Note: You could, however, write an episode in which he dreams of being a super cat with such magical powers. For a clever writer, there are always ways of breaking the rules if your story absolutely dictates it.

Sometimes, a cartooniverse rule will affect the character's dialogue:

Donny from *The Thornberry's* doesn't speak intelligibly while Kenny from *South Park* doesn't speak at all.

As a writer, if you wrote for these series, you would never write dialogue for the characters above.

As you can see, anything goes in the animated world, as long as it is included in the premise of its cartooniverse and the rules remain constant. In *Peanuts*, Lucy is never going to let Charlie Brown kick that football, and Snoopy is never going to behave like a normal dog. And it is exactly because of these rules, that the audience keeps watching.

Road Rule #1: Don't break the rules of the series' cartooniverse!

As a writer, stay within the confines of the cartooniverse's rules. When you step out of these rules, you mark yourself as an amateur.

Animation Fines

Any script that presents difficulty or extra time and effort for the animators (and therefore greater costs to the producer) will be "ticketed" for a huge fine (that is, you can forget selling your spec script or getting a freelance assignment). As an animation writer, you have to be aware of the financial limitations of illustrating what you write. Of course, you'll always find one or two exceptions in the cartoons you watch, but just remember: you are beginning your career. You want to build a good reputation, and believe me, you can't afford to be labeled as writing scripts which cost too much to produce.

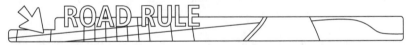

Road Rule #2: No crowd scenes.

You don't need them anyway. Just have a close up on three or four people to represent your crowd.

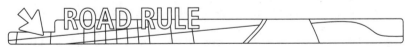

Road Rule #3: Don't remodel set designs.

Backgrounds for the cartoons are established in the pilot episode and those that follow. Thus, these can be reused for every episode thereafter.

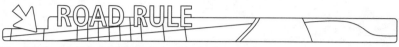

Road Rule #4: Don't add numerous new locations.

It just means creating new backgrounds for a show which already has backgrounds. *The Simpsons* can afford to do this, but Saturday morning cartoons can't. Know the cartoon and the places the characters travel. Use those locations if possible.

If you want to write a *Johnny Bravo* teleplay, then research the show. What locations and sets are already established? Well, there's Johnny's kitchen, den, his neighborhood, Pop's Palace, and the park to name a few.

In *Dexter's Laboratory*, we generally see Dexter's lab, the kitchen, living room, the kid's bedrooms, the neighborhood and/or the school. These locations are pre-existing so use them in your own story.

In *Dr. Katz*, they keep their locations fairly tight. Generally, every episode contains the reception area, Dr. Katz's office, Dr. Katz's apartment (kitchen, den, bedrooms, bathroom) and sometimes the local bar.

Study the show for which you want to write your sample script. Keep a log of the locations and sets it uses over a course of six to eight episodes. When you start plotting your story, try to incorporate as many of these as will work. You are not forced to use these places. Don't feel your creativity is being thwarted by these rules. You just want to prove you know the show, and respect its financial limitations. If you need to add a new location or two, do so. Just don't create an episode which requires half of its locations and sets to be drawn from scratch.

If you're creating a new series, then you don't want to break any of these Road Rules and suffer animation fines either. You want to keep your series' bible as appealing as possible to network or studio executives. This means keep costs low while coming up with a saleable series.

Likewise, if you seek to write a sample script, you won't want to be "ticketed" either. You want your sample script to appear as professional as possible, and illustrate that you understand the rules of the animation business.

Remember, down the road, you will have greater flexibility once you have a track record with the story editors (although once you do get an assignment, always check with your story editors before writing something which adds additional costs). Until then, trust me, don't write a scene in which a hundred robotic insects come buzzing over New York City. You could send the story editor into cardiac arrest just thinking about such costs.

Before we get to our first exercise, there's another road rule you need to know:

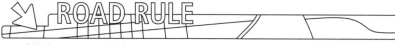

Road Rule #5: Never choose the same series for which you eventually want to write.

For legal reasons, story editors can't and won't read sample scripts written for their own show. They don't want to be accused of stealing ideas submitted to them. (Besides, most of them are honorable people, so don't worry.) Since story editors will generally read work not submitted from an agent, this is protection for them. Choose a cartoon series *similar* to the series for which you would like to write.

Once you finish all the exercises in this book, you will have two sample scripts to show. These scripts will be your calling card. Whichever show you select to write for, make sure you stick with the rules of its cartooniverse so you present yourself as a professional.

Exercise 1: Video tape, then watch three cartoon episodes from *different* series. List every cartoon physical feat . How many feats per cartoon episode did you list?

Exercise 2: Peruse your TV guide or channel surf cartoon stations. List three examples from animated series for each of the following: classic cartoon characters, marquee ideas, and original concepts. (No fair using any listed in this chapter.)

Exercise 3A: Video tape and watch three additional cartoons from the *same* series. Choose a series for which you might be interested in writing one of your sample scripts. What rules do the characters follow in their cartooniverse? List as many as you can observe.

Exercise 3B: If you are creating your own series, do exercise (3A) first to study rules of other series. Next, list the cartooniverse rules for the series you are creating.

Note: Once you get a freelance assignment on a particular show with your sample scripts, then the story editors will send you the series bible so you can get to know their show.

Exercise 4: In each of the six cartoons you have viewed, go back through the episodes and see how many "Animation Fines," if any, occurred in these episodes. (You'll likely find fewer "fines" on the Saturday morning cartoons than on the cable networks.)

Chapter Two
Cartoon Genres – Your Tunnel Vision

Basically, there are seven major types of cartoon genres: action, comedy-action, character, fantasy, gag, sitcom, and spoof. Think of each genre as a tunnel in which the style of animation writing is exclusive to that particular tunnel.

Can genres cross over? Absolutely. You'll have gags in all these genres, after all, they are cartoons. The amount and type of gags, however, will vary from tunnel to tunnel. Examine the overall tone and structure consistent throughout a cartoon series to establish its genre.

1 The Action Tunnel

Action cartoons mean just that - Action! Action! Action! Your teleplay will involve action sequences, building the story and culminating in the story's climax with more action. In an action tunnel, you can't stop your story for numerous gags or character scenes. In fact, the only place for humor in this genre is usually found in the dialogue. You must keep inside the action tunnel, hurling obstacles continuously at the characters, causing them to scramble to solve or escape such obstacles.

This genre often plays to the older audience, ages twelve and up. *Batman*, *Dragon Ball Z*, and *Rescue Heroes* are examples of the action genre.

2 Comedy-Action Tunnel

Comedy action mixes action with witty dialogue and gag humor. A gag is simply a quip, laugh-provoking remark, or visually humorous joke. In this tunnel, you can take time for gags and other types of humor. You have a balance of gag and action sequences.

Usually, these cartoons appeal to the six to ten year old audience, and therefore, the humor must play to this audience's level of sophistication. *Blasters*, *Ace Ventura Pet Detective*, and *C.O.W. Boys Of Moo Mesa* fall into this genre.

3 Character Tunnel

Character cartoons are ones in which the story's main plot line is a character plot line. That is, the story derives from the traits of the serie's characters and their relationships to each other, and therefore is an emotional story line. The audience watches to see what happens to the character. This type of tunnel most often has a moral or lesson plotted within its structure (as we will discuss in Chapter Three).

This tunnel seeks the six and under audience, and is more likely to appeal to girls than to boys. *The New Adventures of Winnie the Pooh*, *Rugrats*, and *The Little Mermaid* fit into this genre.

4 Fantasy Tunnel

In the rules of this tunnel, the characters often fantasize or daydream sequences which are visually shown to the audience. These cartoons have an element of fantasy and imagination in them, and often play to the younger audience as well. This cartoon genre includes shows such as *Doug*, *Muppet Babies*, and *Pepper Ann*.

5 Gag Tunnel

This genre encompasses almost all of the Warner Brothers cartoons. They built their cartoon reputation and animation history on their gags. In this cartoon genre, the story is all about gags, more gags, and topper gags.

This tunnel captures the six to twelve age range, although it can be appreciated by any audience as the humor relies on numerous visual gags. *Tiny Toons*, *Beetlejuice*, and *Courage The Cowardly Dog* illustrate the stylistic writing of the gag tunnel.

6 Sitcom Tunnel

Sitcoms are half-hour shows which almost play as live-action, that is, they are structured like any sitcom in a live-action prime-time series. Their stories often derive from an event or situation which real life families might experience. Shows such as *The Simpsons*, *King Of The Hill*, and *Dr. Katz* depict this cartoon tunnel.

7 Spoof Tunnel

This tunnel makes fun, in a good-natured way, of a well-known person or character. *Inspector Gadget* spoofs Don Adam's detective character from *Get Smart* while *Johnny Bravo* spoofs Elvis. *Mighty Mouse*, naturally, pokes fun at the super heroes, such as Superman. In this genre, the writer must play off of the spoof. That is, the humor comes from the character being an amusing version of a well-known character.

Tunnel Vision

As a writer, decide which genre best fits your writing style. If you're brilliant at writing gags, then perhaps you want to create sample scripts for that cartoon tunnel and therefore, showoff your own unique talents as a writer. It's also important to familiarize yourself with the various shows currently on the air. What is the popular trend? Certainly, animated sitcoms were a tunnel trend in the 1990's. Whichever tunnel you choose, you'll want to write both sample scripts in that genre to demonstrate your skills. Story editors will want to read at least two sample scripts from the same genre as their show to see if you have an understanding of the genre.

Road Rule #6: Whatever genre you choose, remain within its tunnel boundaries.

You must have tunnel vision when it comes to genre. Don't mark yourself as an amateur by writing an action story for *Winne the Pooh* or a gag story for *Batman*.

Exercise 5: Video tape and watch six new cartoons, trying to view different genres. Classify the cartoons by their respective cartoon tunnels.

For the exercise below, choose cartoon series which are presently in production because you want your sample scripts to be current.

Exercise 6: List the genre in which you have chosen to write your two sample episodes. Will this cartoon tunnel show off your skills as a writer? These are your calling cards. Choose the genre best suited for your writing abilities, and the genre in which you wish to work.

Note: Those of you creating your own series, develop one teleplay for your series and one from an existing series on television. It's always good to have a script which illustrates that you can also write for someone else's characters and cartooniverse.

Chapter Three
The Moral or Lesson

For some cartoon series, before you develop your story, you'll need to decide its moral. That is, what does your character learn in the course of the story? Many animated episodes have some moral or lesson taught, even those filled with action such as *Rescue Heroes*. More often, the moral or lesson will appear in plots of 22 minute or 11 minute lengths.

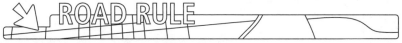

Road Rule #7: Your moral or lesson will be that flashing light in the distance that keeps you on course as you plot your script.

Often, a character will state the moral or lesson, usually in the resolution (the closing of the story) especially in those stories plotted for a younger audience. Spoken aloud or not, your moral or lesson must always be *embodied* in a character who will complete it, just not until the end of the story.

In *The Simpsons, I Love Lisa*, Lisa learns "honesty is the best policy," especially when dealing with someone's feelings. (Implied)

In *C.O.W. Boys Of Moo Mesa, The Legend of Skull Duggery*, young Cody realizes it's not wise to go exploring without telling an adult where he's going. (Stated)

In *Sabrina's Truth or Scare*, the title character learns that accepting dares is stupid and can be very dangerous. (Stated)

In *Rugrats, Moving Away*, Angelica discovers she really will miss her friends, the "babies." (Stated)

Saturday morning cartoons are more likely to have a moral or lesson than those cartoon series on the cable channels. You'll have to survey cartoons to know which ones have morals or lessons incorporated in their shows and their cartooniverse, and which are merely for entertainment purposes.

While the character may learn something, it doesn't necessarily change him. It's more a lesson for the audience than the character. He'll be back to his old habits in the next episode. There's no humor if Charlie Brown learns Lucy is never going to let him kick the ball, and just simply refuses to kick it. And who wants to watch Bart Simpson if he's not up to some kind of prank or if Homer stopped being such a loser and became successful?

Cartoons offer us a safe and familiar world to escape to where things never truly change. Unlike real life, the characters never grow up: their innocence or their cynicism is preserved forever, and that's the way we, as an audience, like

Exercise 7: Choose six cartoons you've previously viewed. Write the moral or lesson learned (if applicable). Was it spoken in the cartoon? If so, by whom? Which character was the moral or lesson embodied

Exercise 8: In the exercises above, did you come across the same moral? If the answer is yes, were the morals found in the same or different genres?

These exercises will help you build your own list of morals or lessons to use. It's also a good way to see how the same moral or lesson can be executed in very different ways and in very different

Exercise 9: Choose six morals or lessons you want to write a story around (three each for the two series you've chosen to write sample teleplays for or three for your own series and three for an existing series). Remember, write both scripts in the same genre.

Note: If the two series you've chosen to write your sample scripts for don't incorporate a lesson in their plots, then skip this exercise and move on to the next chapter.

Chapter Four
The Central Idea

What's next in constructing your literary highway? The central idea. You will develop the moral around a central story idea if your cartooniverse has a moral woven into its plot. If it doesn't, that's okay. You'll just be creating a central idea.

The central idea sums up in a sentence or two who and what your story is about. Set up the idea keeping in mind how long you have to tell your story. In cartoons, there are three basic format lengths: 22 minutes, 11 minutes, and 7 minutes, and your story must fit into one of them. The shorter your structure length, the more simple your plot.

Note: You may see cartoons which range from 30 seconds to 3 _ minutes, but these are almost always written by an animation writer who creates and animates his own story in this format.

First, let's look at those cartoons which do integrate both a moral and central idea, and distinguish between the two:

In *The Simpsons, I Love Lisa*, the lesson is, "Honesty is the best policy." The central idea is Ralph has a crush on Lisa who uses him in order to go to Krusty's 29th Anniversary Show.

In *C.O.W. Boys Of Moo Mesa, The Legend of Skull Duggery*, Cody learns he's not old enough to go unsupervised. The central idea is that the kids find a treasure map and go off to search for silver where they encounter a dangerous ghost.

In *Pepper Ann, Were You Ever Unsupervised?* the title character learns her friends aren't going to judge her if she isn't ready to do certain grown-up things. The central idea is: Dieter throws a party not supervised by adults, and Pepper Ann is nervous about playing spin the bottle.

In *The New Adventures Of Winnie The Pooh How Much is that Rabbit in the Window?* Rabbit learns he is special. The central idea: feeling unappreciated, Rabbit runs away to find a new set of friends.

Okay, now let's look at those episodes which developed their stories only from a central idea:

The central idea of *A Boy and His Bird* (*Johnny Bravo*) is that Johnny discovers dogs can be "babe" magnets, and so adopts a "dog," to get dates. That is, he adopts an Emu he thinks is a dog.

In *The G.I.R.L. Squad* (*Dexter's Laboratory*), Dee Dee and her friends form a crime squad and hunt out crime in their neighborhood.

In *The Baby Sitter*, (*Cow & Chicken*) Chicken tries to survive Cow's babysitting when the parents go out for a night of dancing.

From these central ideas, the writers of each of the examples above executed their plot lines.

The Three Basic Story Plots

Think of the central idea as the fuel which drives your script. Your central idea should be strong and should depict conflict for your characters. It should also be an idea with which the audience can identify. What jeopardy plagues the hero so the audience can relate to his/her plight? You want the audience to park and get into the car with your hero, going along on his/her ride.

So how do you start creating that central idea? Well, remember:

Road Rule #8: All stories come from a variation of the three basic plots the Greeks developed thousands of years ago; man vs nature, man vs. man, man vs. himself.

1 Man vs. Man

2 Man vs. Nature

3 Man vs. Himself

Man vs. Man
In the man vs. man plot line, it often is a fight to the finish.

Survival is our most primary instinct. For a writer, it's that life vs death scenario. Our hero fights it out to the end. The hero's struggle is obvious: If the hero fails, he's dead (or someone he cares about is dead). Most action and action/comedy cartoons depict this plot. *Jonny Quest* (both old and new) *Batman, Dragon Ball Z* (along with most of the imported Japanese animated series) and *Reboot* generally use this type of plot for their stories.

For example, in *Day of the Samurai*, Batman and the Ninja battle to the death.

This plot line, however, can also be about a non life-threatening competition between two or more of the characters. The level of tension and emotion of the story depend on what is at stake.

In *The Penalty Wheel* (*Cow & Chicken*) the title characters compete on a game show against two other characters and the game show host.

Man vs. Nature
The man vs. nature plot line is generally a life or death situation as well. Here, the character struggles with nature's wrath: a storm, a flood, an earthquake, a volcano, a tornado, a hurricane, an avalanche – you get the idea.

In *Rescue Heroes, Cave-In* an earthquake traps a group of school children and geologists inside a cave. The team works to save victims as aftershocks cause dangerous and explosive gases to leak from the earth. The earthquake and poisonous gases serve as the story's villains. This series is dependent on this type of plot line for its episodes.

In *Batman, Day of the Samurai*, Batman battles the evil Ninja (man vs. man) but also must save himself from the erupting volcano (man vs. nature). In this episode, both plot forms were at play. In the 22 minute structure you'll have time to combine two types of plot lines if you need to.

Man vs Himself
The man vs himself scenario is a character type story, and therefore probably would be seen either as a subplot in the 22 minute structure or a plot line in the 11 minute format (which is a character format).

In *The New Adventure's of Winnie The Pooh: How Much is that Rabbit in the Window?* Rabbit creates all his problems by assuming his friends don't appreciate him, and by never asking for their help.

In *Gundam Wing*, through the beginning episodes, Hiro struggles with his duty to the mission and his growing love for Renata, whom he believes he should kill as she knows his secret.

Remember, you aren't coming up with an original plot, so relax. It's easier than you think. If you have trouble coming up with ideas, "borrow" from the classics. A great source of story ideas can be found in fairy tales and fables. Just choose a fairy tale and put a new spin on it. Kids love this.

In *Johnny and the Beanstalk* (*Johnny Bravo*) Johnny trades for some Magic Hair Tonic which grows into a huge "hairstalk." Johnny climbs it to find – you guessed it, a giant. From this series of actions, the story spins its gags.

Exercise 10: Choose three previously watched cartoons. List their central ideas. Compare how the central idea and moral (if there is one) merge together, complimenting each other. Which of the three basic plots did the episodes use?

Exercise 11: Choose the type of plot line you will be using for your own two episodes. (You might use more than one in your story, but one must dominate.)

Exercise 12: Using the six morals or lessons you've chosen to write about (three for each of the two series) formulate central ideas for each. If the series doesn't have a moral or lesson, just develop your central idea. Use ONLY one or two sentences to do so. If you are merging a central idea with a moral, make sure the two are compatible with each other.

Chapter Five
Dead End Ahead – The Central Question

The central question of your story is the focus of your plot, and the question which is answered in the climax (the big clash or confrontation). It dead ends in the last act and all the streets (scenes) you construct will lead into it. On your Road Map, it is labeled "Central Question Avenue".

Road Rule #9: Before you construct your plot, know where your road ends. Knowing the ending of your story will keep you from writing scenes which wander aimlessly in your script, only to be discarded in the rewrite.

In a 22 minute format, Central Question Avenue will be answered in Act Three, in a 11 minute format, in Act Two, and in a 7 minute format, in Act One. Whichever format or structure you use, the audience can't know the answer to the central question until the end of the story.

In *Day of the Ninja* (*Batman*) the central question is: "Will Batman stop the Ninja?" Two other subplots which also have a central question: "Will Batman rescue the kidnaped student," and "Will the volcano consume Batman and/or the Ninja?"

In *The Legend of Skull Duggery* (*C.O.W. Boys Of Moo Mesa*) the central question is: Will Cody, Carly and little Jake find Duggery's treasure and escape alive? One of the subplot's central question is: Will our heroes find the kids in time?

In *Cradle Attraction* (*Rugrats*) the central question: "Will Chuckie survive his first brush with love?"

Since it is an 11-minute format, there is less time to develop a subplot, so there are none for this story.

In *The Unusual Suspects* (*Pepper Ann*) the central question is, "Who stole the school's otter statue?"

You'll also find A-story (your main plot storyline) central questions in the 7 minute format, but none for subplots (your B-storylines). There isn't time to develop any.

The Baby Sitter (*Cow & Chicken*) the central question: "Will Chicken survive a night of Cow's baby sitting?"

The *G.I.R.L. Squad* (*Dexter's Laboratory*) asks the central question: "Will Dee Dee and the girl detectives get their man?"

Exercise #13: Before you develop your own central question avenues, identify those from any six cartoons you've watched. Include central questions for any subplots.

Note: If it's been awhile since you saw them, just watch the last few minutes to refresh your memory. What questions are answered in the story's climax?

Exercise #14: Choose your favorite two central ideas (one for each of the two series). Write the central question for the A-story (main plot line) and for the B-story (subplot) if applicable.

Now, you have the direction your hero will be driving, which takes us to our next chapter.

Chapter Six
Characters

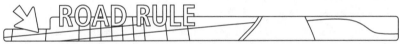

Road Rule #10: If you are developing your own series, be sure to give the audience a driver to care about, and one we can laugh with along the ride.

All cartoon characters must be what executives call, "kid relatable" as most cartoons are targeted for children. Even though the character is animated, he still must have needs and desires as people do. This is what makes an audience relate to the cartoon character, and tune into the series every week. If the characters aren't relatable to their audience, no matter what the age, no one watches them. This means huge financial losses to the networks, studios, and advertisers.

So how do you begin to make your characters relatable? You start by choosing character type.

Types of Drivers

The main character in your story, the protagonist or hero, is the driver of your story. You can separate most cartoon heroes into four categories:

---

1 The Race Car Driver

2 The Taxi Driver

3 The Demolition Derby Driver

4 The Anti-Car Driver

The Race Car Driver

The extraordinary hero is your race car driver, a risk taker who can maneuver out of any situation with his or her awesome talent/talents or powers. S/he excels in his/her environment, never (or rarely) failing. As an audience, this is the kind of hero we admire. He's Bugs Bunny (*Looney Toons*) *Batman* (for most part, any of the Super heroes) or Dexter (*Dexter's Laboratory*). This character speeds along his own course, and the audience lives vicariously through this driver's adventures. Generally, s/he isn't the one who learns a lesson, but often teaches another character the lesson.

The Taxi Driver

The taxi driver is the regular guy/gal who's just like anyone who might get into his/ her cab. As an audience, we can relate to this driver because s/he's one of us. He's the boy or girl-next-door type. Tommy (*Rugrats*) or Pepper Ann (*Pepper Ann*) or Dr. Katz (*Dr. Katz*). Sometimes, he's the character who triumphs outside his capabilities, like Goofy from *Goof Troop* or *Mr. Magoo*.

The Demolition Derby Driver

Another type of hero/ heroin you might choose to tell your story is the demolition derby driver. This character has many handicaps going into the story, and during his/ her journey, s/he's getting slammed from all directions in his/ her beat-up jalopy, always ending up on the bottom of the pile. S/he never (or rarely) triumphs in his/his attempts. Wiley E. Coyote is a classic example as is Charlie Brown. Cartman (*South Park*) and Homer (*The Simpsons*) are others. These characters immediately win the audience's sympathy because throughout the story this character *really* struggles to achieve his/her goal. Fate has not treated this character fairly, and thus, we want to see them win even if sometimes they are their own worst enemy.

The Anti-Car Driver

Last, but never least, is the anti-car driver. This protagonist doesn't embody the usual attributes of a hero or fit into society's norms. S/he's the "bad boy" type (or at least s/he thinks s/he is). S/he doesn't believe the rules apply to him. S/he chooses his/ her own vehicle and drives on his/ her own course (like the race car driver) but his/ her traits aren't ones we as an audience wish to acquire, characters such as Bart (*The Simpsons*) Johnny (*Johnny Bravo*) or Daffy Duck (*Looney Tunes*).

Note: For those creating a series, if you choose to tell your story with an anti-car driver (anti-hero) make sure this character has some kind of universal appeal to which an audience can relate. No matter how incorrigible he/she is, this driver should have some lovable qualities as well. Remember, Bart Simpson does sometimes help his sister, and Johnny Bravo respects his "mama."

Exercise #15: From the previous cartoons you've watched, list the hero type who drives that episode.

Exercise #16: For your own teleplays, list which type of driver you will use?

Goal, Need, Fear & Arc

The most important factors to know about your character:

1 His/her goal and need

2 What he/she fears most

3 His/her character arc

Let's examine each of these.

His/her Goal and Need

You must create your driver with a very blatant goal and need, then put his/ her on a one way street to achieve it. Your driver, no matter which type you choose, must be committed to his/ her goal.

Your hero's goal and need are two separate factors. Your driver's need generally is what fuels the B-story (emotional subplot).

I Love Lisa (*The Simpsons*) Ralph's goal is to win Lisa's affections, while his need is for her to like him.

In *Day of the Ninja*, Batman's goal is to save the hostage and stop the Ninja. His need is to help his old mentor.

In *The Legend of Skull Duggery* (*C.O.W. Boys Of Moo Mesa*) Cody's goal is to find the treasure, but his need is to prove he's too old to be supervised.

In *How Much is that Rabbit in the Window?* (*The New Adventures Of Winnie The Pooh*), Rabbit's goal is to find new friends, but his need is to be appreciated and to feel special.

Even in the 7 minute cartoon structure, you'll find a character has a goal or a need which services the plot, although he/she will rarely have both, due to time restraints.

In *Dexter's Laboratory, G.I.R.L. Squad*, Dee Dee's goal is to catch criminals.

In *Cow & Chicken, The Baby Sitter*, Chicken needs for Cow to leave him alone.

What he/she fears most

A character's fear is sometimes a great element from which to develop a story:

"Homer Simpson in *Kidney Trouble*, Homer's fear of donating a kidney to his father, leads him to flee the hospital, and helps build some of the plot points and emotional lines.

In *Have You Ever Been Unsupervised?* (*Pepper Ann*) her fear of having to maybe kiss a boy at Dieter's party fuels the story line.

In *Garfield & Friends Annoying Things*, his fear of the dog who has threatened him (not to make any more jokes about dogs) fuels the story's gags.

His/Her Character Arc:
What the driver learns in the course of the story is called the character's arc. In Chapter Three, you decided what your driver will learn along the journey, and studied examples of series that had a moral or lesson. Often, a character's fear is useful in constructing a character arc because you can build a story in which the character overcomes his fear, or at least confronts it as in the Pepper Ann example above. This always makes your character vulnerable, and therefore very relatable to an audience. In addition, it can help you plot his/her goal by having the goal be to overcome what the character fears.

Exercise #17: From six cartoons you've previously viewed, write what the driver's goal and need is. Include any fear the driver has that plays into the story's plot (if applicable).

Exercise #18: List your driver's goal and need in each of the two stories you are developing. If you are building a plot around a character's fear, list that as well. You should have already written your driver's character arc (what he/she learns) from the previous exercise in Chapter Three (if applicable). If you haven't, do so now.

Identification Please. Who Is Your Driver?

Ever hear your mother tell you, "Don't get in the car with a stranger?" Well, she's right. You have to know the driver of your story or you won't be able to write him/her convincingly and consistently.

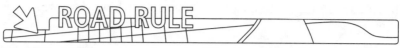

Road Rule #11: Know your characters! You must know the cartoon and its cartooniverse to know how your characters will act and react with one another. Stay consistent to the cartooniverse and its characters.

To write for an existing cartoon series, you'll need to know their characters as if you created them yourself. For those of you who are creating your own characters, you'll follow these two tools as well in developing your characters.

1 Character Dipsticks

2 Character Compass

Character Dipsticks

A dipstick consists of everything you know or have learned about the character for which you are writing. Dipsticks measure the five fundamental characteristics of each character whether he's the driver, villain, supporting character, or sidekick. These five fundamental characteristics include:

1. Is the character's animation superhuman, (*Superman*) human, (*Hey Arnold*) mechanical, (*Inspector Gadget*) or animal, (*Cow & Chicken*) or a toy (Winnie the Pooh)?

If he is mechanical, animal, or a toy does he or she have humanistic traits? Snoopy (*Peanuts*) walks upright, but doesn't speak. Likewise, Garfield walks upright, but does speak although his lips don't move.

2. What is his/her approximate age: pre-kindergarten (the babies of *Rugrats*) elementary (our gang from *South Park*) junior high (*Pepper Ann*) high school (Judy Jetson from *The Jetsons*) young adult (the gang from *Scooby Doo*) or adult (*Dr. Katz*) or elderly (the couple in *Courage The Cowardly Dog*)?

3. Does he/she have super or magical powers? (*Superman* or *Sabrina*)

4. What environment does he/she live in? Is it a futuristic world (*Blasters*) or just every day middle school here on earth (*Pepper Ann*)?

5. What is the driver's relationship to the other characters in the series? Who are his friends? Who are his enemies? Who are his parents? Who are his classmates? You must know how characters relate to each other because their chemistry is very important. Learn their backstory (history with one another) to know how your characters will act and react with one another.

Sometimes the rules of the cartooniverse set the relationship between characters. For example, Wiley E. Coyote is always going to chase the Road Runner, and Lucy is always going to yank that football before Charlie Brown can kick it. Eustas will always be mean to Courage The Cowardly Dog while Muriel will always treat her pet kindly.

Character Compass
Know the character for which you are writing. Whether hero, villain or sidekick, look at the character's world through his or her eyes. See their world through their limited view because each one will have their own POV (point of view).

To learn about the character, watch the series in which he or she appears for at least half a dozen times to discover a character's personality traits. What are the character's strengths and weaknesses? How have these experiences and relationships defined his/her personality? These traits serve as compass points for the character, and direct his/her choices and reactions throughout the journey.

The character's type is his/her "true north." That is, what category he/she falls in will determine how this character moves through the plot. For example:

Homer, a demolition driver, always gets slammed from one angle or another, so this will play into the plot points. Homer Simpson in *Kidney Trouble* depicts Homer generously offering to give his dad a kidney, but when he finds out it is a dangerous operation, he bolts, running off to sea. Yet, even on the *Ship of Lost Souls*, he is an outcast and tossed off. Going back to redeem himself, Homer still can't go through with the operation – he makes a quick getaway again, but this time, he's slammed (literally) by a falling car. When he wakes up in the hospital, he's in traction, and he's missing a kidney.

The fact that Batman falls into the race car driver category means that he will have to have an extraordinary villain to fight because Batman must struggle to win in the story and his traits must be shown off in the story. If the villain is no match for Batman, then the audience will feel cheated, or that the fight was unfair.

Let's examine the drivers and their character compass traits from four of the various series we've discussed thus far:

Batman (Race Car)	Cow (Taxi Driver)	Homer Simpson (Demolition)	Johnny Bravo (Anti-Car)
Intelligent	Sweet	Dumb	Vain
Skilled Athlete	Playful	Lazy	Conceited
Loner	Girlish	Uncouth	Dry Wit
Lonely	Pouty	Cowardly	Playboy
Loyal	Babyish	Whiner	Mama's Boy
Courageous	Imaginative	Family Man	Stupid
Principled	Spoiled	Blue Collar	Loyal

Exercise #19: Create a dipstick for each driver of the two series for which you are writing. Include the five measuring marks, especially noting the relationships and backstory between the main characters in each of the two series.

Exercise #20: Create a character compass for each of the two drivers you are writing about, listing flawed traits as well as good ones. What is the driver's true north?

Pedestrians or Passengers – Supporting Characters & Sidekicks

Supporting characters are those who "support" the driver. These characters illuminate the driver's compass traits and/or further the plot. They also serve to bounce off dialogue and/or they are targets to derive humor. Likewise, sidekicks function the same, except a sidekick is a character who is "attached" to either the driver or the villain, and doesn't really interact with the other characters in the series. Many times, a sidekick will be the driver's or villain's pet.

In *Peanuts*, the supporting cast is: Snoopy, Lucy, Linus, Sally, Schroeder, Peppermint Patty, and Pig Pen. Snoopy's sidekick is Woodstock.

Often it is the villain who has a sidekick. One of my all time favorite sidekicks is Mutley, Dick Dastardly's sidekick (*Wacky Racers*). Mutley rarely supports Dick Dastardly's ornery schemes, laughing when his owner fails.

Pepper Ann doesn't have a sidekick, but the supporting cast includes Milo, Trinket, Dieter, Nicky, and Pepper Ann's mother.

Supporting characters and sidekicks can be more fun to write because they can be less serious or driven than your hero.

Character Tics

Often a cartoon character, whether driver, supporting, sidekick or villain, possesses what is known as a character tic. A tic is a trait or quirk unique to that particular cartoon character, like Sherlock Holmes' famous hat and pipe. Often tics are exhibited in voice distinctions. For example:

The Riddler (*Batman*) speaks in riddles.

Piglet's stutter (*Winnie The Pooh*)

Daffy Duck's lisp (*Looney Toons*)

Donald Duck's unusual and barely intelligible raspy voice (Disney)

The adults speak, "Wah – wah -wah -wah" in *Peanuts*

Johnny's voice mimics Elvis in *Johnny Bravo*

Sometimes, the voice tic may be that the character doesn't speak at all:

Kenny (*South Park*)

Wiley E. Coyote

Pink Panther (in the original series)

Creating characters with distinctive voices obviously helps to identify such a character quickly to the audience. A character tic, however, doesn't just have to be related to a character's speech or voice.

Count Duckula: The title character is a vampire duck who is a vegetarian, and faints at the sight of blood.

Winnie The Pooh: Tigger bounces on his tail.

Peanuts: Linus is never without his security blanket, much to his sister, Lucy's, annoyance.

You should always let a character's tic play into your plot whenever possible. In *Stripes* (*Winnie the Pooh*) Tigger loses his stripes and his ability to bounce. The whole plot is built around Tigger's character tic, and his sadness. Who is he now that he can't bounce?

Exercise #21: List any character tics in the series for which you are writing, and remember them when plotting.

Exercise #22: Create character compasses for the supporting characters and sidekicks. Look for traits which clash with the driver's traits. This will help you develop humor and/or conflict in your scenes. Develop a dipstick for at least three of the supporting characters and/or the sidekick, especially including the backstory and relationship he/she has with the driver of the series.

Road Rage

Ah, villains. Where would our driver be without them? Obviously, in a very boring story. Your hero must have someone or something to race or clash with throughout the story. The villain/hero sets out to achieve a goal and the other one tries to foil that attempt. Villains are driven by their need to control the outcome of your plot. Both your villain and your driver will each have their own respective goal and need. As the writer, your job is to ensure these two goals and/or needs come into conflict.

Types of Cartoon Villains

Basically, there are four main types of villains:

1 Road Rage Driver Villain

2 Aggressive Driver Villain

3 Sunday Driver Villain

4 Vehicle or Open Road Itself

Road Rage Driver Villain
The road rage driver is a villain intent on destroying your hero or others at any cost. That is the villain's main motivation and goal in the story. This type of villain has virtually no redeeming qualities, and serves as an almost unconquerable obstacle for your protagonist.

Freiza and Cell (*Dragon Ball Z*)

Hex (*Reboot*)

Aggressive Driver Villain

This villain acts as a competitor or nemesis for your hero. This villain wants to win whatever your hero and he/she is vying for; a toy, an award, a love interest... They need to be as clever, or more clever than your hero so that when your protagonist defeats this villain, the audience won't feel it was an easy victory, but one well earned.

Dick Dastardly (*Wacky Racers*)

Megabite (*Reboot*)

Roger (*Doug*)

Sunday Driver Villain

This villain is more of an aggravation to your hero. S/he causes irksome delays and situations for your hero/ heroine. Generally, s/he thrives on making your driver's life miserable.

Angelica (*Rugrats*)

Principal Hickey (*Pepper Ann*)

Monty (*Tiny Toons*)

Vehicle or Open Road Itself

This villain often is used as an additional villain to help complicate the climax. This is the driver's vehicle or the open road itself, which means it is either a machine or nature which poses a threat to your hero. For example, the computer software (vehicle) which is loaded in *Reboot*, or the forces of natures (open road) which often cause calamities in *Rescue Heroes*.

Note: Although this book is about half-hour cartoons, it is important to note that some of the most memorable and rotten villains ever created are found in animated features. Cruella De Ville (*101 Dalmations*) Ursula the Sea Witch (*The Little Mermaid*) and Sid (the toy-torturing kid next door in *Toy Story*) are evil and nasty enough to give adults nightmares.

Just because your villains are animated, don't make them any less evil, cruel or ornery.

Some cartoon villains, however, don't see themselves as bad. They have reasons and justifications for the bad things they do.

A great example of the "honorable" villain is Megavolt from *Darkwing Duck*. This villain steals appliances, but not because he wishes to be a thief. His motive is honorable: he seeks to save the enslaved appliances, freeing them from their owners and bringing them to life.

The last factor you need to know about villains is that cartoon series often have a round robin of villains rather than one villain in particular. That is, there are numerous villains to choose from and use in that particular cartooniverse. These villains reappear in various episodes. Often action shows have a round robin of villains. As a writer, if you are writing for such a series, you can pull out one of these villains to use in your own episode.

For example, *Batman* has many enemies: Scarecrow, The Joker, Mr. Freeze, Riddler, The Penguin, and Poison Ivy to name a few.

Exercise #23: List the type of villain your hero fight will against. This could include a new villain you are creating for your episode or one of the round robin villains in the series. Write down your villain's goal and/or need in your story unless using type 4 (machine or nature).

Exercise #24: If using villain types 1 - 3, then create a dipstick for your villain. Next, make the villain's character compass. What is your villain's true north (his type)?

Adding New Characters

Before adding characters to your story, you'll need to take into consideration the resulting animation expenses. While this might not sound costly, remember, this is animation. A new character means extensive drawings, not just one picture. Animation involves a series of movements for a character, therefore, drawings showing how a new character sits, stands, and moves must be completed from the front, back, and profile of a character. That's nine separate drawings at least just to add one new character. Get the picture?

New characters also mean additional actors to lend their voices to the character. This adds more cost to the production. While many actors can create various voices, any one actor usually doesn't do more than three characters in any one series. Therefore, a new actor would have to be hired.

Road Rule #12: Use as many of the serie's own characters rather than adding your own. If you do add a character(s), keep them to a minimum (unless allowed in the rules of its cartooniverse)!

You'll make the animators happy (less work for them) the producer happy (less expense for them) and the story editor happy (who will feel you have a strong sense of the show).

Sometimes, it's all right to bring in a new villain and one sidekick because this helps keep a series fresh and interesting. Watch the series for which you want to write, and follow its example. If it rarely introduces new villains, but uses its own round robin of villains, then follow its lead and do the same.

If the series is a large cast show, don't include all the characters. When you have an assignment, if it is a large cast series, your story editor will generally set a limit.

If you do add a new character, give him/ her a distinctive voice and describe him/ her so you give animators and story editors a character they can immediately hear and see in their mind. For example, "a raccoon bandit who has a Peter Lorre accent."

Note: There is a trick to sneaking in new characters; make them integral to the plot, make them entertaining, and give them just one or two lines in the script because the actor gets paid by the number of lines.

Once you do get a freelance assignment, you can always seek permission from the story editors to add a new character if you truly believe the character is necessary to your story. Until then, its best to follow the Rules of the Road.

Exercise #25: If creating a new character or two, then make them UNIQUE! List their compass traits, true north, dipstick markers, and any character tics (including distinctive voices) they may have.

1. Character Tags:

Once you begin writing the actual script, there is a technical format to follow in regard to characters. When a new character steps onto the page for the *first* time, introduce their name in CAPS and sum them up in a one or two sentence character tag (description) which sticks in the reader's mind. Include any character tics (including distinctive voices or speech patterns). You want a story editor to immediately grasp who this character is in your teleplay.

Look at the following examples of character tags:

Dark Fang: a maniacal wolf with a sinister voice is the meanest hombre this side of the mesa. When opened, his cape creates a frosty wind which freezes his victims.

One-Eyed Jack is a rabid looking Jack Rabbit with one-eye which shoots out a red laser, aging its victims. He wears a patch over the other eye. His raspy voice demands attention.

Exercise #26: Sum up any new character originally in a one or two sentence tag, making each character sound fascinating and distinctive. Create a character tic if you like. You'll use these tags later in the actually script, so do the work here. That way, you won't have to slow your momentum during the first draft of your teleplay when you're focusing on plot.

Just to recap:

1. Know the characters' true north and major compass traits. This will keep you writing the character consistently, and illustrate your knowledge of the series. It will also assist you in knowing how the driver will react in each scene and/or situation. You must insure the characters are driving their own vehicles rather than being bused by you, the writer. Your characters must follow their own needs in the plot, not yours.

2. Make sure each new character you create is unique and fun. Give the character a distinctive tic. Have him/her complement and contrast with existing ones in the series.

3. Characters must be believable to get the audience attached. When creating your own, make the character creditable as well. When writing for existing characters, make them consistent.

Read children's literature for ideas in regards to creating characters kids will love. Examine the classics of children's literature and fairytales. These have endured the test of time for a reason, and they can give you a great sense of story and character.

Chapter Seven
Introduction To Plot

Let's take a look at the basics of plotting a story. The villain must hurl falling rocks (obstacles) into the pathway of your driver regardless which story structure or format (22 minute, 11 minute, or 7 minute) you've chosen to write,. Each falling rock along the journey must cause your driver to react and propel him up a steeper incline. In other words, keep upping the stakes, zooming your driver faster into your story until he's left with only one choice to make at the end to solve the problem.

In your central idea, you decided from whose point of view (POV) your story will be told. In a large cast, remember, it doesn't always have to be from the hero's unless that's a rule of the series' cartooniverse (as is the case in *Batman* or *Johnny Bravo*). Begin thinking of how you will narrate the story. Will it be told straight from beginning to end, or will there be flashbacks? If you're writing a sample script for *Doug*, you must use flashbacks to tell your story because that's one of the rules of its cartooniverse.

In your construction, integrate the plot and the character so each is dependent on the other. The plot is your roadway system, and the hero is the driver zooming down your story's streets. You'll also weave a winding road (subplot) or two, which reflects the main plot, if you are working within the 22 minute structure.

You can use parallel plotting if you like, although you must do so cleverly. Parallel plotting means you're writing the same story in the main plot and in the subplot; it's just seen through another character's point of view.

In *The Legend of Skull Duggery* (*C.O.W. Boys Of Moo Mesa*) Cody wanted to prove to our heroes that he was grown up enough to be one of Marshall Moo's Deputies. In a parallel subplot, Saddle Sore and Boot Hill wanted to prove they were worthy to be Sheriff Terrorbull's lackeys.

In *The Unusual Suspects* (*Pepper Ann*) the main plot is a parallel plot. Principal Hickey "interrogates" Milo, Nicky, Trinket and Dieter. Each section of the plot reveals each character's own version of what happened. It's the same story, just seen through different points of view.

Graphing

The best way to learn the structure of a specific cartoon series is by graphing several of its episodes. By graphing, I mean listing the structure of a cartoon scene by scene as you watch it. Obviously, it's best to videotape the episode, then graph it so you can pause while jotting down your notes. In your graph, list the location, who's in the scene, what is the point of the scene, and any other important information given in the scene. Sometimes, it's helpful to include the line of dialogue that sums up the scene.

Also, note the *real* time the scene occurs in the episode. For example, when does the sixth scene occur? Two minutes into the cartoon? Three minutes? Or maybe even four? This helps you determine the approximate page that scene would fall in the script. It will also guide you when you're structuring story sequences in following chapters.

Road Rule #13: Two animated script pages equals one screen minute (on average).

Below, I have included the graphs of three different cartoon series, each representing one of the three cartoon formats and a different genre. We'll be using these graphs in the following chapters. I chose them randomly, from series which are available for viewing either on television or at the video store.

Graph of *The Simpsons: I Love Lisa*

written by Frank Mula

Format: 22-minute

Cartoon Tunnel: Sitcom

Central A-story Question: Will Ralph win Lisa's affections?

Central B-story Question: Will Lisa "survive" Ralph's courting?

ACT ONE

(1) EXT. RADIO STATION: KBBL, hear "Monster Mash" playing, establish it's Valentine's Day.

(2) INT. BART'S ROOM: Bart paints sayings on candy sweethearts: "Eat My Shorts" "U Stink" etc...

(3) INT. REST HOME: Grandpa bummed when his friend gets a Valentine's card and no one sends him one.

(4) INT. MOE'S BAR: Moe gets Secret Admirer Card from crude guy at bar.

(5) INT. KITCHEN: Marge serves Homer a special breakfast. Bart tries to get Homer in trouble as Homer's forgotten it's Valentine's Day, although he pretends he remembered.

(6) EXT. BACKYARD: Next door, Flanders serenades his wife.

(7) INT. KITCHEN: Homer lies, says he has gift upstairs, and flees the room.

(8) INT. MINI-MART: Homer buys box of chocolates for $100.00 as clerk sees he is desperate for a gift.

(9) INT. SCHOOL, LISA'S CLASS: Kids make mailboxes for their Valentine cards. Kids laugh at Ralph because he's being nerdy. Intercom:

(10) INT. PRINCIPAL'S OFFICE: Principal Skinner announces someone ("probably Bart") wrote obnoxious sayings on candy. Valentine's Day is not a joke.

(11) FLASHBACK TO DA NANG JUNGLE: 1969, President Skinner remembers when buddy was killed on Valentine's Day.

(12) INT. BART'S CLASSROOM: Bart proud of his prank.

(13) INT. LISA'S CLASSROOM: Everyone exchanges Valentines, no one gives Ralph one and his feelings are hurt. Feeling sorry for him, Lisa gives him a card. Ralph's enamored now. (6 minutes into the episode)

(14) INT. LUNCHROOM: Bart excited for special mystery meat being served./INT. LUNCHROOM KITCHEN: Unloads gross meat on dirty floor.

(15) INT. LUNCHROOM: Bart plays prank- fake baboon heart.

(16) EXT. SCHOOL: Ralph asks to walk Lisa home. They reach her house and she rushes inside to escape him.

(17) INT. DEN: Homer and Bart watch the "Itchy & Scratchy" show. See a clip from the show. Krusty the Clown comes on and announces he is having his 29th Anniversary show soon. Bart and Homer really want to go.

(18) INT. KITCHEN: Lisa seeks advice from Marge on how to make Ralph understand she doesn't like him without hurting his feelings. Homer comes in for a beer, and gives his advice.

(19) EXT. PLAYGROUND: Lisa tells Ralph that she's not ready to date.

(20) INT. RALPH'S KITCHEN: Ralph seeks advice from his father, the cop. He says be persistent. Ralph decides he won't give up! (9 minutes into the episode)

ACT TWO

(21) INT. DEN: TV screen shows Krusty, four days until his show. Lisa and Bart desperate to go, but no way they can get tickets. Doorbell rings. It's Ralph! Lisa hides from him. Homer answers.

(22) INT. BACKYARD: Homer uses Ralph's desire to date his daughter, making Ralph do chores around the house.

(23) INT. SCHOOL: President's Day Play tryouts. Teacher chooses Ralph to play George Washington to Lisa's Martha Washington.

(24) EXT. SCHOOL PARKING LOT: See Ralph's dad ordering his cops to take off tow-truck boot – he's blackmailed the teacher into giving Ralph the part.

(25) INT. DEN: Lisa upset, worries Ralph will embarrass her in the play. Doorbell. Ralph's left Lisa a gift, a Malibu Stacey Convertible. In its trunk, two tickets to Krusty Show. Bart's envious, he'll go in her place with Ralph.

(26) INT. LIVING ROOM: Lisa asks Homer whether or not to go, is it ethical since she doesn't like him? Homer says, it's Krusty! Go!

(27) INT. POLICE CAR: Ralph's dad takes Ralph and Lisa to the show. Tells how he got tickets. FLASHBACK EXT./INT. PORN MOVIE THEATER: Ralph's dad goes in to catch the film when sees Krusty there – pretends he's going to bust Krusty.

(28) INT. POLICE CAR: Lisa doesn't think that's an appropriate story to tell them.

(29) INT. KRUSTY SHOW: Krusty shows clips, talks to the audience. Ralph spills ice cream on Lisa, Lisa prays she's not shown on TV sitting with Ralph. Ralph professes his love for her on TV. Mortified, Lisa shouts she doesn't like him! She just gave him the Valentine's Day card because no one else would, and she just went on a date with him so she could see the Krusty Show.

(30) INT. DEN – LATER: Bart and Lisa watch the fiasco on video. In the replay, Lisa sees Ralph's face as she yells - she's broken his heart. Lisa feels miserable. (18 minutes into the episode)

ACT THREE

(31) EXT. PARK: Ralph feeds the ducks as his dad tries to cheer him up.

(32) INT./EXT CAR: Ralph's dad pull Homer over and gives him a bogus ticket because Lisa has hurt his son.

(33) EXT./INT. SCHOOL: Refreshments being served as play begins.

(34) INT. AUDITORIUM: Play begins with tribute to the lesser known presidents, a musical number.

(35) INT. BACKSTAGE: Bart moons his fellow thespians. He's playing John Wilkes Booth. Lisa tries to apologize to Ralph, but he won't speak to her. Teacher directs Milhouse, who's playing Lincoln, onto stage along with Bart who shoots him. Then has to pull a zealous Bart off the stage.

(36) INT. ONSTAGE: Ralph looks at the Valentine Lisa gave him, uses it to fuel his emotions. He performs brilliantly as the dying George Washington. Reactions from audience, impressed.

(37) BIG FINALE: Mt. Rushmore lowered onto stage as the stone presidents speak. Play ends.

(38) EXT. SCHOOL: Ralph signs autographs, he's beaming. Lisa swings nearby, tells Ralph he was really good in the play. Ralph joins her. She gives him a card that asks to be friends. Ralph gleeful. They swing and talk.

(39) INT. POLICE CAR: Ralph's dad watches them nearby in his car, happily. On the radio, hear "Monster Mash" playing. (27 _ minutes into the episode).

Graph of *Rugrats: The Word of the Day*

written by Vinny Montello & Steve Ochs

Format: 11 minute

Cartoon Tunnel: Character

A-story central question: "Will Angelica get to be the new helper on Miss Carol's television show?"

ACT ONE

(1) INT. DEN: Angela watches "Miss Carol's Happy House," Tommy interrupts. Draw names for new kid to audition to be Miss Carol's helper on her show. Angela hears her name called. (Intercuts with the TV show.)

(2) EXT./INT. TV STATION: Kids audition, Angela auditions as well. Her mom's proud, gets phone call. Angela sees Miss Carol go into her dressing room.

(3) INT. DRESSING ROOM: Assistant comes into the room. Angelica eavesdrops from the hallway. Miss Carol says a "fun" phrase (only it's really a swear word). Angela thinks she has the scoop on the other kids because she knows the new word.

(4) INT. DEN: Mom watches with the babies and Angelica – her name is announced as a finalist. New helper announced. Angelica needs the best dress. Angelica's excited. Tells mother fun phrase. She is shocked by the word. She must explain to Angelica that the word is "bad."

In the playpen, the babies can't figure out how a word can be bad.

(5) INT. DEN – LATER THAT DAY: Parents explain about the bad word, never to say the word again. Angelica trying to figure out which is the bad word. She starts to say it - SMASH CUT TO:

(6) EXT. HOUSE – Workman jackhammers - we don't hear the word.

(7) INT. ANGELICA'S BEDROOM – NIGHT: She cries, now she can't go audition. (7 – minutes into the episode)

ACT TWO

(11) INT. KITCHEN: Angela coaxes her parents into letting her audition, promising never to say the bad word again.

(12) INT. TV STATION: Assistant gives the kids the new fun phrase. Angela rushes in late, not hearing the new fun phrase, "Swell-o-matic."

(13) INT. TV STATION: Go on air. Parents watch proudly in the audience. The two kids before her freeze up in the on camera audition. Angelica auditions. Miss Carol asks her what the fun phrase is. Angelica hesitates, then says the bad word again on television. Parents mortified.

(14) INT. DEN: Relatives watching, their reaction.

(15) INT. TV STATION: Miss Carol furious, Angelica explains she's just repeating what Miss Carol had said the day before. Miss Carol loses temper and screams the word again.

(16) INT. TV STATION – AUDIO BOOTH: Technicians shocked as they cut off the air.

(17) INT. TV STATION – Angelica glad Miss Carol admits saying the bad word.

(18) EXT. HOUSE/INT. DEN: Babies watch the show, only now it's Miss Stephanie's Happy House show. Parents won't let Angelica be new helper. Babies try to comfort her. (11 minutes into the episode)

Graph of *Dexter's Laboratory: G.I.R.L. Squad*

written by Rumen Patok

Format: 7 minute

Cartoon Tunnel: Fantasy

A-story central question: Will Dee Dee and her detectives get their man?

ACT ONE:

(1) INT. SCHOOL AUDITORIUM: McBark the Crime Dog, boring speaker, gives speech about crime, shows slides. Dex is the projectionist.

(2) EXT. SCHOOL: Dee Dee and girls form detective squad, ala Charlie's Angels. MUSIC MONTAGE They are ready to "lick" crime.

(3) INT. TREE HOUSE: Dee Dee searches out crime, spots jaywalker.

(4) Dee Dee chases the jaywalker through the city, catches up with him.

(5) EXT. TRUCK: Dee Dee hitches a ride back to her neighborhood with the jaywalker in tow.

(6) EXT. NEIGHBORHOOD: Joins her detectives. Licks jaywalker. They say they don't think she should actually lick him to lick the crime. Dee Dee not sure what McBark mean. They should ask Dexter.

(7) INT. DEXTER'S LAB: he shows them various crime gadgets, then dumps them from his lab.

(8) EXT. LAWN: Girls hunt for more criminals. Logo shown as they spot a new suspect. Follow him. Follow him again.

(9) EXT. NEIGHBORHOOD: Girls warn neighbors of suspect.

(10) EXT. NEIGHBORHOOD: Girls snatch evidence (really just neighbor's stuff they are collecting)

(11) INT. TREE HOUSE: Girls go through the "evidence", spot suspect entering Dee Dee's house. Panic.

(12) INT. HOUSE: Dee Dee asks mother where the "murderer" went.

(13) EXT. BACKYARD: Dee Dee and girls attack criminal as he cuts down their tree house. It crashes. Neighbors gather. McBark arrives. Criminal is just the gardener. Crime solved.

Exercise #27: Study the graphs above. Once you're familiar with the process, graph 3 episodes from each of the three structure formats: 22 minute, 11 minute, and 7 minute. Any genre is fine. Be sure to include when each new scene begins (in real time) as you will need this data for the exercises in the following chapters.

In the next chapter, we'll examine the major plot points inherent to each of these animation formats. Now, the real construction begins.

Note: If you are writing your sample scripts in the 11 or 7 minute formats, do not skip Chapter Eight: the 22 minute format. It discusses terms you will need to know in Chapters Nine and Ten as well as includes exercises you should complete.

Chapter Eight
The Twenty-Two Minute Structure

This structure follows the same story structure as a feature film only with fewer complications. Usually, this format contains both an A and B story. The A-story line is the main plot while the B-story is most often the character line, however, the B-story can be another action subplot which winds through the story. Action, action comedy, and sitcom genres follow the 22 minute format. Cartoon series which use this format include *The Simpsons*, *Reboot*, *C.O.W. Boys Of Moo Mesa*, *Batman*, *Ace Ventura Pet Detective*, and *Dr. Katz*.

In the 22 minute format, you have about 44 pages to plot. More than 48 pages is too long while less than 40 pages is too short. There are three acts which break into a 9 minute act (18 pages) a 7 minute act (14 pages) and a 6 minute act (12 pages). Generally, Act One is the 9 minutes act, but sometimes it's reversed, and Act One is the 7 minute act. It depends on your story, however, your shortest act should always be Act Three.

Remember, an animator will be adding gags or images to your teleplay which will lengthen the timing of your script as well.

Road Rule #14: In animation, the animator will interpret the visual aspects of your script, but it's your job as a writer to send him in the visual direction you want him to go.

Think of your plot as a series of streets which merge into Central Question Avenue. Each street on the Road Map equals one scene or a sequence of connected scenes like in a music montage or an action sequence. You create a new scene whenever you switch time (going from morning to night) or location (going from inside the house to outside the house) in your story. Each set of streets (or scenes) forms one city block. Thus, in a 22 minute structure:

Teaser = 1 – 2 streets (if applicable)

Act One = 1 city block (the set-up)

Act Two = 1 city block (the complication)

Act Three = 1 city block (climax & resolution)

In this format, there will be a Ramp (act out) at the end of each city block. An act out is the scene which precedes the commercial break. These Ramps must accomplish one or more of these **Six Story Signposts:**

1 The driver (hero) has to make a choice.

2 It keeps the audience guessing about the outcome of the central question.

3 It shifts the story down a new road.

4 It makes the road more hazardous for the driver.

5 Takes us into a new arena (locale or setting)

6 It must speed the story into the next act.

Note: These signposts are derived from the turning point's functions Linda Seger lists in her book *MAKING A GOOD SCRIPT GREAT*. I highly recommend this book for your writer's library.

Okay, it's time to get the characters into the plot. To fill those terrifying blank pages, never fear! All you need is your Road Map.

Road Rule#15: Your opening scenes are crucial! Think visually! Think action! The cartoon starts with the 1st frame on the TV screen. Start with an action or a gag!

Your audience is comprised of kids who play video games and/or adults who channel surf. Both have very short attention spans. Hook them from the beginning, whether it's in the Teaser or the opening of Act One.

Teaser

A teaser is an opening scene or sequence which "teases" the audience into staying tuned and not switching the channel. Sometimes a series uses a teaser and goes to a commercial break, whereas other series use a teaser then go to their main credits, then back to the show. Either way, it functions the same: to grab and hold the audience's attention. If the series you are writing for has a teaser, make it exciting, and leave your driver facing a calamity or dilemma.

In *Cave-In* (*Rescue Heroes*) the team rescues the crew of a boat during a storm in the Pacific.

In *Sound Advice* (*Blasters*) G.C. is trying to eat with chopsticks, causing havoc. The chef races out at her, angrily.

In *Mystery of the Dancing Ghost* (*Anatole*) the children read a ghost story, then suddenly they hear a noise – It's the ghost!

Road Map (see page 188)

Note: It's okay if you don't fill in every street on your Road Map or have an extra street in one of your city blocks. This is just a guideline. Use them only if your story requires them.

Exercise #28: Using a brief sentence, fill in ONLY the 1st Street on your Road Map whether it's a Teaser or the first scene in Act One. Make it exciting.

Act One

Act One consists of 1st- 20th Streets, and introduces all the elements needed to tell your story without giving away all your story. There are three important plot points you must construct in Act One:

1 The Tow-Away Street

2 The Green Light

3 On Ramp

Tow-Away Street

This street is your catalyst, it's what happens to spin the story. The Tow-Away Street is where your driver (hero) is towed or pulled into the story, whether or not he wants to be. This street spins the central question of the main plot (A-story). In a mystery, it's usually the crime. In an action or action comedy, this is often the scene or street when the villain appears. This street can also be found in the teaser of the story. You don't want to stall; you've only got 22 minutes to tell the story which means you should tow your driver into the story within the first four minutes (that is, by page 8).

The Simpsons – Sitcom: In *I Love Lisa*, the Tow-Away Street is when Lisa gives Ralph a Valentine. All the action from then on derives from this catalyst. (3 minutes into the episode)

C.O.W. Boys Of Moo Mesa – Action comedy: In *The Legend of Skull Duggery*, it's when Cody, Carly and Jake find a treasure map in Miss Kate's Attic. (4 1/2 minutes into the episode)

Batman – Action: In *Day of the Samurai*, it's the kidnapping of the martial arts student. (1 minute into the episode)

The Green Light

This street is where your driver (hero) hits the gas and zooms into the action; he commits to the conflict. He might not want to, but he must! In a sitcom, the Green Light usually occurs on the same street as the On Ramp (act-out). In an action or action comedy genre, it most likely falls about half-way through Act One, or shortly after the catalyst.

The Simpsons, I Love Lisa, the Green Light flashes when Ralph vows to keep trying to win Lisa's affections. He has made a commitment to the plot. This falls on the same street as the On Ramp. (9 minutes into the episode)

C.O.W. Boys Of Moo Mesa, The Legend of Skull Duggery,: Cody decides to go after the silver on Skull Mountain. This falls about midway through Act One. (4 minutes into the episode)

Batman, Day of the Samurai, the Green Light occurs on the street in which Batman declares he's going to Nipan to help his old Sin Say. This occurs early in Act One, just after the catalyst. (2 minutes into the episode)

On Ramp

At 20th Street, the end of Act One, there must be more at stake for your driver. This is the scene which precedes the commercial break. In the sitcom tunnel, the driver most likely faces an emotional hurdle, or has a new resolve to achieve his goal. In an action or action-comedy tunnel, the driver must always be left with a crisis: S/he, or someone s/he cares about is in jeopardy. This On Ramp, 20th Street, must incorporate several of the six story signposts (p.66.)

The Simpsons I Love Lisa: Ralph declares his intention to keep courting Lisa even though she's told him she doesn't want to date. (9 minutes into episode). Includes signposts: 1, 2, 4, 6.

C.O.W. Boys Of Moo Mesa: Jake disappears into the mine yelling – Skull Duggery's got him! (7 1/2 minutes into the episode) Includes signposts: 2, 3, 4, 5, 6

Batman: Batman confides to Alfred that the Ninja knows Bruce Wayne and Batman are the same man, and seeks to kill him. (6 1/2 minutes into the episode) It includes signposts: 2, 4, 6

The examples above depict very different genres, but the basic plotting contains the three important plot points of Act One.

Exercise #29: Examine the cartoon you graphed for the 22 minute format. What is its central question? List the Tow-Away Street, Green Light, and On Ramp (20th Street). What signposts occur on 20th Street? At what time in the episode did each occur?

(Hint: Think about the central question. What is answered in the story's climax? Only the scene which truly zooms your driver in that direction can qualify as the Tow-Away Street.)

If the two series you have chosen to write for work within the confines of the 22 minute structure, then you can now start plotting your first story (either for existing series or creating your own). If you are writing the 11 or 7 minute structure, continue reading, and only work the *odd* numbered exercises in this chapter.

Note: Those writing the 22 minute structure, complete all the exercises in this chapter before beginning your second script's Road Map.

Exercise #30: Choose one of your stories from the six central ideas you developed previously. Fill in your moral, (if applicable) central idea, and central question on the Road Map Form. Also copy the goal and need of the hero and the villain onto the form. Each of these elements will give you a direction for your plot. List the Tow-Away Street and Green Light. Next fill in On Ramp, 20th Street. Make sure it contains several story signposts. Is your driver's goal serviced by these major plot points of Act One? It should be.

Act Two

Caution! You must sustain the tension throughout this city block. This city block encompasses 21st – 30th Streets. In the action or action-comedy tunnel, Act Two generally opens with resolving the immediate danger of the driver or the friend of the driver, and then continues the plot. In the sitcom tunnel, the story picks up where it left off.

As your driver travels through the story, s/he must have enough Falling Rocks (obstacles) to complicate his/ her efforts. Regardless of genre, as the driver speeds to achieve his/ her goal, the antagonist wrecks or attempts to wreck the hero's actions by hurling these rocks. You will hurl a few rocks at your driver in Act One, then really toss them across his pathway in Act Two.

In the 22 minute format, Act Two has two major plot points:

1 The U-Turn

2 No Outlet Ramp

The U-Turn

This is the midpoint of Act Two. It turns the story in an unexpected direction, raising the central question again so the audience keeps guessing about your story's outcome. It also raises the stakes or jeopardy for the driver. The U-Turn must be strong enough to fuel the second half of Act Two.

In *I Love Lisa* (*The Simpsons*) the midpoint occurs on the street where Ralph gives Lisa a tempting gift – two tickets to the Krusty Show, if she'll come as his date. (13 minutes into episode)

In *The Legend of Skull Duggery* (*C.O.W. Boys Of Moo Mesa*) it's the scene Duggery suddenly appears, startling the kids, and causing them to fall into the swift river. Now, unlikely they will find the silver, and they have a bigger problem – they're lost in the mine with an evil ghost, and they didn't tell anyone where they were going. (12 1/2 minutes into episode)

In *Day of the Samurai* (*Batman*) it's when Batman recovers the hostage, but the Ninja escapes with the map which tells the location of the scroll describing the deadly martial art. (3 minutes into episode)

No Outlet Ramp

The No Outlet occurs on 30th Street. It is the Ramp for your Act Two – the ROAD OF NO RETURN. Act Two culminates on 30th Street. It must place your driver in more jeopardy or calamity than in the Act One On Ramp. If it doesn't, you have a story with an incline that's falling rather than rising.

On the No Outlet Ramp, there is no going back. Your driver must drive onto this street with some threat to himself or to someone he cares about, or with some consequence to his achieving his goal. He makes a conscious choice to enter the action "full speed ahead" and zooms into the motion of the story's climax. The final crash (confrontation) is now inevitable. The question set up on Central Question Avenue will soon be answered in Act Three.

In Act Two, you have increased the Falling Rocks while reducing your driver's choices of escaping these hazards until he hits 30th Street, where there is but one choice left to accomplish his goal.

Let's look at the No Outlet Ramp, or 30th Street, in our examples:

I Love Lisa: It's the scene where Ralph confesses his love, but Lisa rejects him on television. (16 minutes into episode)

(Signpost 1) Ralph chooses to tell everyone he's in love with Lisa.

(Signpost 3) It shifts the story down a new road: Ralph won't be chasing Lisa anymore.

(Signpost 4) It makes the road more hazardous: emotionally, Ralph is now hurt; he's been rejected by Lisa on national television.

(Signpost 5) It switches arenas or settings: Now the story shifts from Valentine's Day and the date, to President's Day and the play.

(Signpost 6) It speeds the story into the next act: What is Lisa going to do to mend Ralph's hurt feelings?

The Legend of Skull Duggery: Cody, Carly and Jake are locked in an anteroom in the mine as the evil ghost floods it! (17 1/2 minutes into episode)

(Signpost 1) The driver must make a choice: What are Cody and the kids going to do to escape their predicament?

(Signpost 2) It keeps the audience guessing about the outcome of the central question: Will the kids escape Duggery?

(Signpost 4) It makes the road more hazardous: Now the kids are literally up to their necks in trouble.

(Signpost 6) It speeds the story into the next act: How are the kids going to get themselves out of this one?

Day of the Samurai: Batman learns the Ninja has kidnapped Alfred. (17 minutes into episode)

(Signpost 1) Driver makes a choice: Batman agrees to fight Ninja.

(Signpost 2) Keeps audience guessing: Will Batman or the Ninja win?

(Signpost 4) The road is more hazardous now that Alfred's life is also in jeopardy.

(Signpost 6) It does speed us into the next act to see how Batman saves Alfred and defeats the Ninja.

All three different genres build rising inclines and increase their story's speed limit as they move towards their climax. Notice how in each example, 30th Street heightens the story to include several signposts. Try to use as many signposts on your No Outlet Ramp as possible.

Exercise #31: From the 22 minute cartoon episode you graphed in the last chapter, list its U-turn and No Outlet Ramp. What time did these scenes occur in Act Two? List the story signposts that fall on No Outlet.

Exercise #32: Now, list your U-turn and fill in on your Road Map your No Outlet, 30th Street. List all the signposts your 30th Street encompasses. If it only uses one or two signposts, rework it to make your act-out stronger and more effective.

The Ticking Clock

As your script progresses, your story's speed limit increases, compressing time shorter until real time for your characters often becomes reel time. This brings us to the need of the "ticking clock." A ticking clock sets into motion an action which must be carried out by a certain time. It differs from a falling rock because of this time demand. This device can help build tension in Act Three, although where you set it in motion depends on your story. Generally, it's found at the end of Act Two, on 30th Street.

Batman's Day of the Samurai: it's the volcano threatening to erupt. It is introduced in the opening of the episode, but starts smoking near the end of Act Two.

C.O.W.Boys Of Moo Mesa's The Legend of Skull Duggery: The water rising in the anteroom where the kids are trapped. This scene is the No Outlet Ramp.

Hey Arnold's Career Day: It's when the boss threatens the Jolly Olly ice cream man. If he doesn't sell all the ice cream by sundown, he is fired.

Exercise #33: List any ticking clocks from the twelve cartoons you viewed earlier. Be sure it is a true ticking clock, and not just a falling rock (obstacle).

Exercise #34: List any ticking clock you want to use in your story.

Act Three

This is your 31st – 40th Streets. This city block builds the climax & resolves the story. It is your easiest act to construct because you already know your ending. Here, the A-story and B-story streets merge into the climax. The climax is the scene the audience anticipates throughout the cartoon. In an action and an action-comedy tunnel, it must be packed with action as the driver and villain crash in a final clash.

The climax in our episode examples:

I Love Lisa: The President's Day Play.

The Legend of Skull Duggery: Moo and heroes save the kids from the flooding anteroom! Moo and Duggery fight it out. Moo escapes just before the mine collapses on Skull Duggery.

Day of the Samurai: The martial arts fight between Batman and the Ninja as the volcano begins erupting near them.

The resolution is where you tie up your story's plot lines and the lesson/ moral is learned. In the last remaining scenes, you allow the hero and other characters to absorb all that has happened to them.

I Love Lisa: Lisa gives Ralph a new card, asking him to be her friend. Ralph is happy and the friendship blooms again.

The Legend of Skull Duggery: The kids are safe at Miss Kate's, and Cody apologizes for not telling anyone where they were going, and biting off more than he could chew.

Day of the Samurai: Batman explains to Alfred how he survived the Ninja's death touch. He says good-by to his old Sin Say.

Exercise #35: List the climax and resolution in the episode you graphed for the 22 minute format.

Exercise #36: List the climax and resolution for the story you are developing.

The Overall Plot

Now that you've created your major plot points throughout your story, it's time to scrutinize the rest of the streets on the Road Map.

In your story, each city block (act) will have its own beginning, middle, and end, just as your script. Within each city block, your speed limit increases and your story constantly rises up a steep incline, making your driver's road more difficult to navigate.

Let's study the Act One city block of *I Love Lisa* (*The Simpsons*):

Establish it's Valentine's Day, Ralph doesn't get a Valentine. Feeling sorry, Lisa gives him one so he won't feel left out (beginning). Ralph then falls in love with Lisa, and walks her home. Lisa avoids Ralph as he tries to court her. Introduce Lisa wants to go to Krusty's 29th Anniversary show. Lisa asks Marge how she can let Ralph know she doesn't like him without hurting his feelings (middle). Lisa tells Ralph she isn't ready to date. Ralph seeks advice from his dad and decides he won't give up on Lisa (end). (Act One plays for 9 minutes)

Now let's examine the Act Two city block of *Day of the Samurai* (*Batman*):

The set-up is made to exchange the pupil for the map. Batman meets the Ninja. He helps the pupil escape, but is tricked by the Ninja who escapes with the map (beginning). Ninja searches for the ancient scroll and finds it. He tears it up. Batman finds the torn scroll, but the Ninja has left. Sin Say worries. Ninja now knows the death touch. Scientists evacuate from volcano site. Batman meditates as Ninja learns the new martial art (middle). Ninja kidnaps Alfred. Batman agrees to fight the Ninja, more determined to stop the Ninja's reign of terror (end). (Act Two plays for 7 1/2 minutes)

Likewise, we also have a beginning, middle, and end among our Act Three sequence as illustrated in *The Legend of Skull Duggery, C.O.W. Boys Of Moo Mesa*:

Moo and our heroes arrive to save the boys (beginning). Moo and Skull Duggery battle it out. Moo escapes just before the mine collapses on Skull Duggery (middle). The kids have a snack while Moo reprimands them. Cody realizes he was wrong to go off on his own (end). (Act Three plays for 5 minutes)

In addition, there are two other factors you'll need to consider when plotting: your winding roads and your rest areas.

Winding Road

The winding road is your subplot. As it winds through the story it must reflect the main plot. You can plot two or three short subplots or have one major subplot. Just follow what your story naturally dictates.

I Love Lisa: the subplots include Homer forgetting to buy Marge a present, Krusty's 29th Anniversary show coming up, and the President's Day play.

The Legend of Skull Duggery: one of the major subplots is Boot Hill and Saddle Sore trying to find the silver first, and get a promotion from Sheriff Terrorbull.

Rest Areas

Although risks are rising, each city block also needs rest areas. You must have breathing space for your characters and for the audience so they can refuel before facing more falling rocks and dangerous curves. Rest area scenes provide character moments or comic relief in the story. For example:

In *Day of the Samurai*: The character moment with Alfred and Batman where Batman confides to Alfred.

In *I Love Lisa*: Bart's Valentine Day pranks and the musical number in the play.

Exercise #37: List any winding road(s) in the 22 minute episode you graphed. Also look for a rest area scene and list it. Is it a character moment or comic relief?

Exercise #38: List any winding road or subplot(s) you wish to construct. Include its Central Question Avenue if it is a major subplot. Make sure your subplot reflects your main plot.

On your Road Map, remember, each street represents one scene or a series of *short* scenes. Write one sentence per street to note the crux or point of each scene.

Exercise #39: Highlight or list all the falling rocks hurled at the driver in the 22 minute episode you graphed. How many are there? How many of the rocks are hurled by the villain directly? How many develop from the situation itself?

Exercise #40: Fill in the rest of the streets, starting with Act One on your Road Map. Use your A-story and B-story central questions to keep you on track. Introduce a reflecting subplot during Act One. Make sure each city block (each Act) has its own beginning, middle and end. Have your villain hurl enough falling rocks in the pathway of your driver. Be sure your speed is increasing (the tension) and your incline is rising (the stakes or jeopardy).

Walla! For those of you working the even exercises, you have just completed your first 22 minute outline.

The Pit Stop Principle

Now that you've done the work, it's time to apply the Pit Stop Principle. This means, pull over and rest. Put your outline aside for at least three days and DON'T TOUCH IT! Think about your story, *really think about it*, letting everything you've read so far sink into your thought processes. Not rushing at this point will save you a good deal of restructuring later, trust me.

When you go through the checklist below, you want to view your Road Map with fresh energy and fresh eyes. The beat outline is where you want to catch your structure mistakes. It's much easier to catch weaknesses (crumbling streets) here, than in your script where you'll have 44 pages through which to tread. Taking this pit stop will save you lots of rewriting later.

Exercise #41: For those writing teleplays for the 11 or 7 minute structure, go now to Chapter Nine, and complete only the *odd* numbered exercises.

Road Map Checklist

Before repeating the even exercises in this chapter for your second script, check your first Road Map for any flaws using the criteria below.

1 Is your opening an attention grabber?

2 Does your Tow-Away Street set-up your central question?

3 Have you given your driver a blatant goal and/or need?

4 Is your hero actively driving along his/ her plotted streets? S/he can't be a passenger in the story!

5 Does your driver "hit the gas" and zoom into the plot at the Green Light?

6 Is your villain's goal in opposition with the driver's goal and/or need?

7 Do your On Ramp and No Outlet Ramps exhibit several signposts? Do both lead us into the next act and towards Central Question Avenue?

8 Does your U-Turn (midpoint) sustain Act Two, spinning the driver in an unexpected direction?

9 Is your No Outlet Ramp stronger than your Act One On Ramp? If you are writing for the action or comedy-action tunnel, does this On Ramp leave your driver in jeopardy? If you are writing for the sitcom tunnel, does this act out leave your character with a crisis or a dilemma?

10 Is your story's incline (jeopardy or stakes) rising?

11 Is your driver's commitment rising as well? As your story progresses, there should be fewer roads (choices) for your driver to take to reach his/ her goal.

12 Are there enough falling rocks (obstacles) for your appropriate genre? Highlight the falling rocks you have created. Do you have enough to sustain the audience's attention?

13 If you have a ticking clock, is it ticking? Did you truly set it into motion?

14 Do you stop for a character moment or some comic relief rest areas? And are these on appropriate streets for your story?

15 If part of the rules of your cartooniverse, does your plot prove your moral or lesson? Is this moral or lesson embodied in the driver who fulfills it in your story's climax?

16 Is your story's climax satisfactory? If you are writing for the action or comedy-action tunnel, is the climax full of action that is bigger than the rest of the action in your story?

17 Do your winding roads (subplots) reflect the main plot?

Exercise #42:

A. Does your Road Map (outline) pass every checkpoint listed above? If you answered no to any checkpoint question, rework any scenes necessary to fix your crumbling streets. If you answered yes to every checkpoint, then continue.

B. Choose another central idea from your five remaining ideas. Repeat the even exercises in this chapter, outlining your next story. Once you've finished, take a Pit Stop. Then go through the checklist for your second Road Map and reconstruct any streets you need.

Congratulations! You have structured two 22 minute outlines. Now the fun really begins.

Chapter Nine
The Eleven Minute Structure

This format falls into a Two Act structure with two city blocks consisting of about 22 scripted pages.

Teaser = 1 street

Act One = 1 city block (the build-up)

Act Two = 1 city block (the climax & resolution)

In this format, both the action (A-story) and the character (B-story) plots are combined and belong to the same character because you only have 11 minutes to tell your story. Here, you won't have time for a subplot, just a rest area or two.

The 11 minute format is most often the character driven structure, but it also can include other genres. Quite often, this format plays to the six year old and under audience. Examples of cartoons with this format include *Rugrats*, *The New Adventures Of Winnie The Pooh*, *Pepper Ann*, *Doug*, and *PB & J Otter*.

Teaser

If you do have a Teaser, it will fall on the very first street and run about thirty seconds to a minute. The Teaser will then be followed by a commercial or by the show's main credits.

Act One

The first act is the build-up, and consists of two thirds of your story (7 minutes or 15 pages). This will be 1st- 10th Streets on your Road Map. In Act One, think of your driver as going up a very steep incline. S/he can't see over the hill until s/he reaches the top. In the 11 minute format there are three important plot points as well:

1. Tow-Away Street

2. Green Light

3. U-Turn

Let's examine how these plot points play in the 11 minute format.

Tow-Away Street
Just like in the 22 minute format, you will also have a Tow-Away Street which functions the same – it is what spins your story.

In *Word of the Day* (*Rugrats*) it's when Angela's name is called on "Miss Carol's Happy House" show. This scene spins the story. (2 minutes into the episode).

In *Doug's Dog's Date* (*Doug*) it's the opening scene as Doug flashes back, telling the audience that there's something wrong with his dog, Pork Chop. (30 seconds into the episode).

In *The Unusual Suspects* (*Pepper Ann*) it's the crime: someone has stolen the Hazelnut School's otter statue. (30 seconds into the episode)

Green Light
This is the next plot point in Act One. Just as in the 22 minute format, it is the street or scene in which your hero drives into the plot. In this structure, it most often occurs in the scene following the Tow-Away Street. In our examples, the Green Light occurs in the following scenes:

The Word of the Day: Angelica auditions to be Miss Carol's helper on the show. Here, she commits to the plot. Until now, she just *reacts* to the story line rather than taking action in it. (3 1/2 minutes into the episode)

Doug's Dog's Date: Doug trails Pork Chop, via 1940's detective style, to find out what is going on with his dog. (1 1/2 minutes into the episode)

The Unusual Suspects: She fears a frame up, and also in 1940's detective style, rehashes the case in flashbacks. (1 1/2 minute into the episode)

U-Turn

What flips us into Act Two, is the U-Turn. It must spin the story in an unexpected or surprise direction. Unlike the 22 minute format where the U-Turn falls in Act Two, in the 11 minute format you'll find it falls in Act One. There is no On Ramp (act out) as the end of the 11 minute Act One is not followed by a commercial break. Here, the commercial break comes between the two separate episodes (two 11 minute episodes make up the half hour).

Note: Sometimes you will find in the 11 minute formatted series, that some stories might run 14 minutes due to additions made by the animator. It will then be followed by a 7 minute episode to make up the half hour.

In our examples, the U-Turn can be found in these scenes:

The Word of the Day: Angelica says the bad word again after her parents have forbidden her to do so. Parents tell her she can't go to the final audition. (7 1/2 minutes into episode)

Doug's Dog's Date: Doug awakes to find Pork Chop has packed and moved after Doug had given him an ultimatum. (7 1/2 minutes into episode)

The Unusual Suspect: Principal Hickey narrows suspects down to one: Pepper Ann, and calls her to his office. (7 1/2 minutes into episode)

The U-Turn Street is a great place to set your ticking clock in motion (if you have one) as in *Hey Arnold, Career Day.*

Exercise #43: Examine the cartoon you graphed for the 11 minute format. What is its central question? List Tow-Away Street, Green Light, and U-Turn. At what time into the episode did each occur?

Road Map (see page 190)

Exercise #44: For those writing in the 11 format, choose one of the six central ideas you developed previously. Fill in your lesson, central idea, and central question on the Road Map Form. Also copy the goal and/or need of the driver, and the goal of the villain (if applicable). Each of these elements will give you a direction for your plot. Now list your Tow-Away, Green Light, and U-Turn Streets. Make sure your driver's goal is being serviced by these major plot points of Act One.

The Overall Plot

Again, each city block has a beginning, middle, and end just as your whole teleplay does. Within these city blocks, as your speed limit increases, your story constantly rises up a steep incline, making your driver's road more difficult to navigate. Falling Rocks will occur, but there won't be as many nor will they be as drastic as in the action genre. Keep your protagonist driving ahead toward Central Question Avenue and the climax.

Let's look first at the Act One sequences (city blocks) of our episode examples:

The Word of the Day: Angelica's name is called on the show, she auditions, eavesdrops on Miss Carol and hears the "fun" phrase (beginning). Angelica tells her parents the phrase. Shocked, they seek professional advice on how to handle the situation. They forbid her to say the word again, she is confused (middle). Later Angela says the bad word again, and her parents forbid her to go to the final audition (end).

Doug's Dog Date: Something strange is going on with Pork Chop. Doug trails his dog, trying to find out (beginning). Doug discovers Pork Chop's in love, helps his dog get ready for his first date. Doug misses Pork Chop while the dog is out on date (middle). Pork Chop's late, and Doug worries. He gives Pork Chop an ultimatum, must choose between Doug and the cute poodle. Next morning, Doug awakes to find Pork Chop's packed and gone (end).

The Unusual Suspect: The Hazelnut School otter statue is missing, and Principal Hickey lists his suspects. Pepper Ann fears a frame-up (beginning). Principal interrogates Dieter, Trinket, Nicky and Milo (middle). He has one suspect left, just who he always suspected – Pepper Ann. He calls her to his office. She enters (end).

Notice how each city block's beginning, middle and end leads into the U-Turn, sending us in an unexpected or surprising turn. By the end of the sequence, the driver reaches the peak or crest in the road, and is just about to start that downhill run.

In Act One, you might have one or two rest areas which give a character moment or provide comic relief, but you won't have time for more than this.

The Word of the Day: The babies try to figure out how a word can be bad.

Doug's Dog's Date: Doug fantasizes what it would be like to have a new pet, a pet lobster.

The Unusual Suspect: Here, there isn't time for a rest area as we have a parallel plot going on: each suspect tells his/her version of what happened, and the humor is found within the different versions.

Act Two

Consisting of 11th – 18 Streets, this act forms the climax and the resolution. It involves about one-third of the story (3 1/2 minutes or about 7 pages). Here, your driver zooms over the peak in the road, and the story speeds downhill as if your driver has no brakes, merging into the climax. Unlike the 22 format where the climax is packed with action, here in the 11 minute format, the climax usually involves an emotional punch or surprise.

Let's take a look at the story climaxes in our episode examples:

The Word of the Day: Angelica rushes to the final audition. Parents watch the show proudly waiting for Angelica's moment. When asked what the fun phrase is, she says the bad word again on television. Her parents are mortified. (Punch)

Doug's Dog's Date: Doug rushes home, realizing he wasn't fair to Pork Chop. He hopes to find his dog and does – Pork Chop's been dumped by his girlfriend who's with another dog. (Surprise and punch)

The Unusual Suspects: Principal Hickey accuses Pepper Ann, giving his version of what he thinks happened. Pepper Ann tries to defend herself when Principal Hickey's secretary returns with the statue. He forgot he asked her weeks ago to take it to be cleaned. (Surprise)

Here, like in the 22 minute, the resolution ties up the story's plot lines, and generally includes the moral or lesson learned (if part of its cartooniverse). It is the last street in your Road Map, allowing the characters to reflect on what has happened or the lesson learned in the course of the story.

The Word of the Day: Angelica doesn't get to be Miss Carol's helper, but the babies try to cheer her up.

Doug's Dog's Date: Everything's back to normal with Pork Chop. Doug realizes friends have to stick together.

The Unusual Suspects: The case is solved, and they all learn it's best not to jump to conclusions.

Notice even though Act Two is very short, it still has a beginning, middle and end within its own block.

Exercise #45: A. In the 11 minute episode you graphed, highlight any obstacles or falling rocks the character faces in the course of the story.

Exercise #46: Fill in the rest of the streets on your Road Map. Use your central question to keep you on track throughout Acts One & Two.

Exercise #47: If writing for the 22 or 7 minute structure, continue now to Chapter Ten.

Note: It's time for a Pit Stop. Skip at least two days before continuing to the next exercise if you are structuring the 11 minute format.

Road Map Checklist

Before repeating the even exercises in this chapter for your second 11 minute script, check your first Road Map for any flaws, using the criteria below.

1 Is your opening an attention grabber?

2 Does your Tow-Away Street set-up your central question?

3 Have you given your driver a blatant goal and/or need?

4 Does your driver "hit the gas" and zoom into the plot at the Green Light?

5 If you have a villain, is s/he hurling falling rocks at your driver?

6 Do you have enough falling rocks (obstacles) to build Act One? Highlight the falling rocks you have created. Do you have enough to sustain the audience's attention?

7 Does your Act One sequence have a beginning, middle and end that puts your driver speeding to the top of that incline?

8 Is your story's incline (jeopardy or stakes) rising?

9 Is your driver's commitment rising as well? As your story progresses, there should be fewer roads (choices) for your driver to take to reach his goal.

10 If you have a ticking clock, is it ticking? Did you truly set it into motion?

11 Does your U-Turn at the end of Act One spin the story in an unexpected or surprise direction?

12 Are your character moments emotional or touching, and/or your comic relief rest areas funny? And are these on appropriate streets for your story?

13 If part of the rules of your cartooniverse, does your plot prove your moral or lesson? Is this moral or lesson embodied in the driver who fulfills it in your story's climax?

14 Is your story's climax satisfactory?

Exercise #48:

A. Does your Road Map pass every checkpoint listed above? If you answered no to any checkpoint question, rework any scenes necessary to fix your crumbling streets. If you answered yes to every checkpoint, then continue on.

B. Choose another central idea from your five remaining ideas. Repeat the even exercises in this chapter. Once you've finished, take a Pit Stop. Then go through the checklist for your second Road Map and reconstruct any streets you need.

Yabba Dabba Do! You have just completed your first 11 minute outlines. Let the fun begin!

Chapter Ten
The Seven Minute Structure

The 7 minute structure generally uses the fantasy, gag or spoof tunnel, all of which are driven by the gags of the plot. It quite likely will play to the six through twelve year old audience. Examples of cartoon series which employ the 7 minute format include *Johnny Bravo*, *Dexter's Laboratory*, *Cow & Chicken*, *Garfield & Friends*, *Courage The Cowardly Dog* and *Tiny Toons*.

In this format, you put your character into a situation on the Tow-Away Street and let him/her zoom through to the finish. You only have an A-story in this structure because that's all you have time to develop. The plot is also a gag driven plot, that is, each gag furthers the plot, merging gag and plot together, until the last street or scene. Most often, the driver's goal or need in the story will be determined from his/her compass traits.

For example, Johnny Bravo is a playboy, so he is motivated by the same goal in most every episode – to impress some cute "babe."

Likewise, Dexter is always up to something in his laboratory, so often the situation drives from his experiments. In *Don't Be A Baby*, Dexter wants to go to an action movie, but his dad says Dexter isn't not old enough – he can go when he's older than his dad. Dexter goes down to the lab to "age" himself and his sister, Dee Dee, so they can go to the film.

Let's break it down specifically:

Act One

This act encompasses the whole story, consisting of 14 pages. Its only city block contains about 15 streets. The three major plot points of this act include:

1 Tow-Away Street

2 Green Light

3 The Topper

Tow-Away Street

Just like in the other formats, this street spins the story, but it must be a situation which can play out in just 7 minutes. It will occur on the first street (and the first minute) of your Road Map as there is no time to lose. Let's look at the Tow-Away Street from the following cartoons:

Cow & Chicken, The Baby Sitter. Their parents want to go out for the evening, but have forgotten to call a babysitter.

Johnny Bravo, Ape Is Enough: Pop asks Johnny to come along and help out on the boat on his trip to the islands.

Dexter's Laboratory, G.I.R.L. Squad: McBark the Crime Dog gives speech at school.

Green Light

Again, the character drives into the action of the plot on this street. In a 7 minute format, there's no driving slow. Your driver comes to the Green Light immediately following the Tow-Away Street in this format. For example, the Green Light for these episodes occur:

The Baby Sitter. Cow starts acting like the baby sitter, and plops Chicken into a high chair beside dolls, trying to feed him.

Ape is Enough: Johnny decides to go with Pop and Carl to the island tropics to do a little native girl watching.

G.I.R.L. Squad: Dee Dee and her girlfriends form the G.I.R.L. Squad.

The Topper

On the last street of your Road Map, comes the topper. In a 7 minute format, the topper is your story's climax. It's the last gag in the story.

ROAD RULE

Road Rule #16: Make sure your topper is funny - leave 'em laughing.

Whereas, in the 22 minute format action genre, you must keep topping the action, throughout the 7 minute format, you keep "upping" the gag. Simply put, you have to top your last gag by making it funnier than the gag before it. Let's inspect the gag/plot sequences from our episode examples.

In *The Baby Sitter* (*Cow & Chicken*):

(1) Cow puts Chicken in a high chair and tries to feed him along with rest of Cow's baby dolls. Chicken gets fed up (pardon the pun) and leaves the table to watch TV.

(2) Cow asks if he's done his homework. Chicken becomes more annoyed, completing the stacks of books. Once again, Chicken tries to watch TV.

(3) Suddenly, Chicken's snatched up by Cow and plopped into a bubble bath with Cow's dolls.

(4) The last humiliation comes when Cow puts a diaper on Chicken and wants a good night kiss.

(5) The topper comes when the parents return to find how responsible Cow's been in his baby-sitting endeavors. Thrilled, they leave Cow in charge as they rush off to Barbados for a two week vacation. Chicken screams in agony.

In *Ape Is Enough*" (*Johnny Bravo*):

(1) Johnny steers incorrectly and smashes into the island.

(2) Natives capture Johnny, making him a male "sacrifice."

(3) A female version of King Kong appears, snatching Johnny.

(4) Ape has crush on Johnny.

(5) Carl's beaten by Ape in fight.

(6) Pop makes Ape – "Ape Wonder of the World"

(7) Ape gets jealous of models taking picture with Johnny

(8) Topper: Mom saves Johnny by singing the beast – and Johnny to sleep.

In *G.I.R.L. Squad* (*Dexter's Laboratory*):

(1) Girls form detective squad (Charlie's Angels homage).

(2) Dee Dee chases jaywalker as if the kid where a major criminal – then licks crime, that is licks kid.

(3) Dexter shows them Bond type tools to catch criminals.

(4) Tail van – tie cans on suspect's van.

(5) Tails suspect – ties cans on suspect's feet.

(6) Gathers evidence – by "borrowing" items from the neighbors, including a cat, in case they are tracking a "cat burglar."

(7) Criminal arrives in house and mom lets the "murderer" inside.

(8) Criminal saws tree house (detective base) down.

(9) Topper – McBark arrives, criminal revealed: he's just the friendly neighborhood gardener. This crime's been licked!

Exercise #49: Review the 7 minute episode you graphed earlier. List its Tow-Away Street and Green Light. Next list the gag/plot sequence, ending with its Topper.

Exercise #50: If you have chosen to write for a 7 minute format, choose one of your six central ideas. On your Road Map, fill in the Tow-Away (1st Street) and the Green Light (2nd Street). Next, fill in your own plot/gag sequence. Complete it with the Topper. Make sure your Topper is funny and makes an effective climax.

Exercise #51: Those writing for the 22 and 11 minute formats, continue now to Chapter Eleven.

Time for a Pit Stop. Take a day off, then go through the checklist below.

Road Map Checklist

Before repeating the exercises in this chapter (only those which focus on developing your Road Map) for your second script, check your first Road Map for any flaws in your outline using the criteria below.

1 Is your opening a grabber?

2 Does your Tow-Away Street set-up your central question?

3 Have you given your driver a blatant goal and/or need?

4 Does your driver "hit the gas" and zoom into the plot at the Green Light?

5 If you have a villain, is he hurling falling rocks at your driver?

6 Do you have enough falling rocks (obstacles) to build Act One? Highlight the falling rocks you have created. Do you have enough to sustain the audience's attention?

7 Does your gag/plot sequence build with each gag topping the one before it?

8 Does your Topper truly top all the gags in the episode or sufficiently pay it off?

Exercise #52:

A. Does your Road Map pass every checkpoint listed above? If you answered no to any checkpoint question, rework any scenes necessary to fix your

crumbling streets. If you answered yes to every checkpoint, continue to the exercise below.

B. Choose another central idea from your five remaining ideas. Repeat all the even numbered exercises in this chapter. Once you've finished, take a Pit Stop. Then go through the checklist for your second Road Map and reconstruct any streets you need.

Hey, hey, hey! You have just completed your two 7 minute outlines. Let the fun begin!

Chapter Eleven
Make 'Em Laugh

What is the most important element of cartoons? Cartoons exist to, "make 'em laugh, make 'em laugh, make 'em laugh." As animation writer, your job is to continuously fill the television screen with something comical. Although cartoon series can be educational, they will always yield to entertainment. Thus as an animation writer, when in doubt:

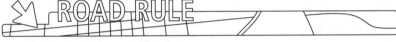

Road Rule #17: Always yield to humor.

While your goal is to write great gags, you want the humor to derive naturally from the plot and/or character.

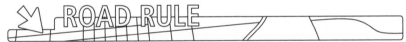

Road Rule #18: The comedy must play to the scene. It must keep moving the story.

Okay, so how do you write humor? Ah, let us count the cones.

Comedy Cones

Think of these as mechanisms of humor, although unlike true traffic cones, they don't signal caution, but comic relief. Comedy cones can assist you in creating humor for your script. Drop them numerously along the streets of your cartoon.

1 Alter Egos

2 Characters In Drag

3 Food Gags

4 Hot Topics

5 Inventions

6 Marquee Humor

7 Musical Numbers

8 Names and Places

9 One-Two-Payoff

10 Parody

11 Physical Feat Gags

12 Play A New Character Opposite of What's Expected

13 Play On Nursery Rhymes or Fairy Tales

14 Potty Humor

15 Props

16 Rule of Three

17 Running Gags

18 Set-Up, Then Payoff

19 Shock-Value

20 Sound Effects (SFX)

21 Surprises

22 Titles

23 Toppers

24 Try-Fails

25 Use of Classic Cartoon Character Gags

Alter Egos
An alter ego is just a second character derived from the original character. Alter egos allow characters to do things they normally

couldn't do. By using this comedy cone, you can break the rules of the character's cartooniverse – and get away with it.

Snoopy's alter egos include: WWI Flying Ace, Tennis Pro, Joe Cool, and Referee.

Cow's alter ego is Super Cow.

South Park plays a variation on this mechanism by having an alternate universe, where the characters are quite the opposite of themselves. Chef is no longer a heavy-set black man, but a skinny white man, and Cartman is not complaining, but nice.

Characters In Drag
Cartoon characters who cross-dress are sure to get a laugh. Warner Brothers loves using this comedy cone. In fact, if there is a "drag queen" of cartoons, it's Bugs Bunny.

In *Hare Conditioned,* Bugs dresses as a customer looking for a pair of shoes.

In *Southern Fried Rabbit,* Bugs disguises himself as a Southern Belle who deceives the Yankee, Yosemite Sam.

Beetlejuice dons a dress and becomes *Bettyjuice* in various episodes.

Food Gags
This type of gag is always popular, especially with the younger audience. The more disgusting or crazy the food concoction, the better.

Cow feeds Chicken marshmallow soup. (*The Baby Sitter*)

Beetlejuice pours a can of concentrated bug bait for his breakfast. (*Bad Neighbor Beetlejuice*)

Wilma Flintstone makes a cactus berry pie with cactus in it. (*Hawaiian Spy*)

Hot Topics
This comedy cone mocks hot topics or current events. Kids are fairly sophisticated today; you'll be surprised what jokes they can understand. Don't write down to them. Cartoons which often employ this comedy cone include *South Park* and *The Simpsons.*

One episode mimics the JFK assassination as Mr. Garrison waits in the Book Depository to shoot guest visitor Kathy Lee Gifford because he knew it wasn't really Kathy Lee, but an alien in disguise. (Revisited in *South Park – City on the...*)

Inventions

The use of inventions is always a good way to bring gags to your scenes.

In fact, often a series will have an inventor character to provide wacky gadgets for the show. That way, there's a built in comedy cone.

As always brain control devices work well. Here, the device reeks havoc on the characters, builds the plot, and lends humor in the episode *Under the Big Flop* (*Johnny Bravo*)

Tigger invents a machine that does everything in order to ease the work load of his friends. It harvests for Rabbit (but of course, damages most of the crop) snatches honey for Pooh (sends bees chasing after Pooh and his friends). Tigger's invention provides most of the plot and humor of this episode. (*The New Adventures Of Winnie The Pooh – Tigger is the Mother of Invention*)

The villain, Illitera, use a camera which shrinks her photographic subjects to minute size. (*Blasters – The Supreme Commander of the Universe*)

Marquee Humor

This humor derives from a sign or book title that the character views or reads in the cartoon scene.

Cow reads from book, "How To Love & Care For Your First Jackal." (*Cow & Chicken – Night of the Ed!*)

Buster Bunny reads from his *Rent-A-Friend* manual in *Tiny Toons* episode *Rent-A-Friend*.

The bus driver views a video manual on what to do when the bus crashes. (*South Park – City on the...*)

Musical Numbers

Having a character break into a song and dance unexpectedly is a great comedy cone (which the *Looney Toon* gang love to use). Musical numbers or montages also add humor.

The play begins with a song and dance about the lesser known presidents. (*The Simpsons – I Love Lisa*)

As the girls form their detective squad, it's shown visually in a music montage. (*Dexter's Laboratory – G.I.R.L. Squad*)

Tigger sings how to clean the room. (*The New Adventures Of Winnie The Pooh – Cleanliness Is Next To Impossible*)

Names and Places
When creating a character, make their name funny as well. Poke fun of or give a flair to names and places.

Larry Lava and Ptrans Pteryalactyl Airlines (*Flintstones – Hawaiian Spy*)

The children's (mice) names are Claude, Claudette, George, Georgette, Paul, Paulette in *Anatole*.

Professor Granite, a geologist (*Rescue Squad – Cave-In*)

One-Two-Payoff
This gag incorporates an action-reaction, and then an unexpected action. Probably the most famous use of the one-two-payoff mechanism is found in *Jaws*. (Excuse me while I digress to a film example, but it so brilliantly illustrates technique.)

In the film, this comedy cone is used for suspense first, humor second. From the first shark attack, eerie music is set up. The audience is now conditioned to expect the killer shark every time the music plays (sort of like Pavlov's dog & salivating). Once we hear that haunting chorus, we cringe – here comes the shark! What makes this film masterful in its suspense is sometimes the music plays, but there is no shark, and sometimes we don't hear the music, then wham! Some unsuspecting swimmer is a shark's snack.

Like in the example above, this technique builds tension because it creates a subconscious suspicion with the audience. The writer jumbles the audience's expectation so that they don't know what is going to happen next. In animation, the suspense is played for humor.

The set up is the one-two which can be played out as many rounds as you have time for, then the payoff comes, only now the audience won't know how it's going to play out. Let's look at animation examples:

In *The Flintstones – Hawaiian Spy*:

(1) As a stuntman, Fred surfs a giant wave, then crashes on the beach(action – reaction)

(2) Next, the director wants Fred to wrestle a dinosaur – The dinosaur attacks, and Fred flees (action - reaction)

(3) The dinosaur chases Fred, and runs past Wilma who punches the dinosaur (payoff – unexpected action)

The example above illustrates the one-two-payoff and uses that magic rule of three (see comedy cone #16).

Parody
A parody is merely a comical or satirical imitation of someone or something. Audiences love it when the cartoon pays homage to celebrities or famous literary characters. Jack Nicholson, Jay Leno, and Elvis are often parodied in cartoons. It also fun to parody well known products.

Note: You can't list a brand name product in your script, that's called "product placement." You can, however, parody a brand name.

Parody of Charlie's Angels plays in Dee Dee's detective Squad and McGruff Crime Dog becomes McBark Crime Dog. (*Dexter's Laboratory – G.I.R.L. Squad*)

Babs Bunny becomes "Babzilla"- a parody of Godzilla, obviously, as she plays during bath time. (*Tiny Toons – Bunny Daze*)

Parody of Don Adams is found in the characters *Inspector Gadget.*

Physical Feat Gags
A. These are gags such as defying gravity and/or other universal laws of physics:

Hang time, a classic Warner Bros. gag, is where the character races off the cliff, then hangs in mid-air with his legs spinning or a character reaction.

X-ray machine reveals Grandpa Simpson has no kidneys, they've burst, and yet he's still alive. (*The Simpsons* – Homer Simpson in *Kidney Trouble*)

Courage's teeth come completely out of his mouth, fall onto the floor, and bounce around chattering. (*Courage The Cowardly Dog* – *Hunchback of Nowhere*)

B. Body distortion: is a gag in which the character's body is distorted or twisted, then returns to normal as if nothing happened.

Cow and Chicken's eyeballs are stretched about a foot from their eye sockets, and literally glued to the television screen they watch. (*Cow & Chicken* – *Night of the Ed*!)

Courage takes off his eyes (which are flat) and wipes them as if they were glass lenses, then puts them back on to get a better look. (*Courage The Cowardly Dog* – *The Gods Must Be Goosey*)

Dee Dee stomps her foot on Dexter's small foot which reacts like the pedal of a trash can and Dexter's mouth pops open 180 degrees (like a lid of the trash can). (*Dexter's Laboratory- Topped Off*)

Play A New Character Opposite of What's Expected
This comedy cone is great for introducing new characters. For example, take a vampire character, and make the character squeamish of blood – and a vegetarian, as seen in the title character *Count Duckula*.

In *Hey Arnold*, the Jolly Olly ice cream man is anything but jolly. In fact, he yells at the kids and throws ice cream bars at them.

Play On Nursery Rhymes or Fairy Tales
Here, you can take an classic story and parody it for a fresh twist.

Instead of beans, Johnny trades for magic hair tonic which grows a magic hairstalk outside the window. (*Johnny Bravo* – *Johnny and the Beanstalk*)

Potty Humor
Anything associated with bodily functions falls into this category. This type of humor mechanism is largely found on cable networks in series such as *South Park*.

The first graders pee in the pool every time Cartman tries to swim to the deep end during their swimming lessons. This is also a running gag in this episode. (*South Park – Summer Sucks*)

(Taking this comedy cone to the extreme, *South Park*, actually created a character made of poop, named Mr. Hanky.)

Props
Use the environment. Always have a lot of props in your script. To further use this comedy cone, use the prop in an unexpected way. Remember, this is animation – you can have a prop appear whenever a character needs one, especially in the gag, fantasy, and spoof genres. It doesn't have to be logical (unless logic is a rule of the cartooniverse).

Daffy pulls on the doorknob, but it shoots out like a knob on a candy vending machine. Later, Daffy pulls on the stairs which react like Venetian blinds, folding shut and forming a slide.

(*Merrie Melodies – A Birth of a Notion*)

Wilma and Betty write a post card, chiseling on rock slab, and a pteryadactyl serves as the airplane. Wilma goes to freshen Fred's makeup for the next film shot, lifting up a baby kangaroo who stomps in the powder, then rapidly pats Fred's face with the powder. (*Flintstones – Hawaiian Spy*)

Buster Bunny wears a "friendship meter" which functions just like a taxi meter. (*Tiny Toons – Rent-A-Friend*)

Rule of Three
Three is the magic number in cartoons. When you write a gag, sometimes you'll want to multiply it by three, that is, repeat the gag three times.

Using the running gag mechanism (comedy cone 17) Wilma burns the Brontesaurus steaks three times during the show: at the beginning, middle, and end. (*Flintstones – Hawaiian Spy*)

Bugs pulls out a gun (Prop) and fires, the flag comes out. It reads: "Bang." The villain shoots. A flag pops out. It reads: "Ouch" (Topper). (*BUGS BUNNY – Hare Conditioned*) This is repeated three times in a row.

Running Gags

A running gag can run through the entire episode or through the entire series. It doesn't necessarily have to be repeated three times, but you can combine it with the above comedy cone if you like.

Kenny gets killed every episode (*South Park*)

Lucy never lets Charlie Brown kick the football (*Peanuts*)

Eustas's eyeballs shoot out from his sockets several feet at Courage, terrorizing the little dog. This gag plays several times in the episode. (*Courage The Cowardly Dog – Hunchback of Nowhere*)

Set-Up, Then Payoff

This is a gag which you set up somewhere in the episode, then pay it off before the end of the episode.

Homer flees the hospital, stopping in front of an oncoming trailer truck. The truck, carrying cars, stops in the nick of time. The audience relaxes, whew! That was a close call. Then one of the cars rolls off and falls onto Homer. (*The Simpsons – Homer Simpson in "Kidney Trouble"*)

Shock-Value

This comedy cone is most often used in series on non-networks such as Comedy Central, the Cartoon Network, and FOX.

The kids are too noisy on the school bus, so the Bus Driver slams the brakes, takes out a bunny rabbit and a pistol, pointing it at the rabbit. She threatens to shoot the rabbit if the kids don't shut up. (*South Park – City on the...*)

Homer and Bart watch "Itchy and Scratchy" on TV, and as its title, "My Bloody Valentine" states, it is bloody and gory as the mouse pulls out the cat's heart. (*The Simpsons – I Love Lisa*)

Sound Effects (SFX)

With this comedy cone, play with the audience's expectations. Put a sound effect where the audience isn't expecting that particular sound or a sound at all.

The group holds a seance. As they stare at the crystal ball, Shirley summons the afterlife: we hear a dial tone, and the scene cleverly plays as if they are conversing on the phone. (*Courage The Cowardly Dog – Shirley the Medium*)

In *Under the Big Flop* (*Johnny Bravo*) ominous music plays in background for the audience to alert us that danger's coming, but the characters in the cartoon make reference to it.

Surprises
Using this mechanism, you place something unexpected or randomly in the scene.

Morning finds Dexter's parents frantic, thinking there is no coffee to wake them up. The mother opens the cabinet, and a arm shoots out holding a coffee can. Juan Valdez sits on a shelf in the cupboard, his donkey beside him. (*Dexter's Laboratory – Topped Off*)

Monty screams into cell phone. A tongue shoots out of the receiver to give the raspberry. (*Tiny Toons – Rent A Friend*)

Lovers run to embrace, but just before they get to each other, the planet explodes. (*Dragon Ball Z – Trouble on Arlia*)

Titles
The audience's first smile, chuckle or laugh can come from your cartoon episode's title. By using any of the other comedy cones, you can develop a comical title for your script.

Snot Your Mother's Music – Pepper Ann (Potty humor)

Under the Big Flop (pun) and *Johnny and the Beanstalk* (fairytales) – *Johnny Bravo*

Stark Raving Dad, Much Abu About Nothing, and *Homer Alone The Simpsons* (parodies & pun)

Toppers
A topper "tops" off the gag, that is, the audience laughs (hopefully) at the first gag, but isn't expecting anything more. Then comes the topper – which should provide an even bigger chuckle or laugh.

At the robotic can-can show in the saloon, the robot's buttocks fly off as the robot dances. The "butt cheeks" land on the bar beside Grandpa Simpson. He pinches them (the gag). A pause. Then, the robot's hand flings off, and as it flies past Grandpa Simpson, it slaps him (the topper). (*The Simpsons* – Homer Simpson in *Kidney Trouble*)

Try-Fails

Here, a character tries and fails, then tries and fails again, over and over either throughout the episode or throughout the series. You want to keep building the gag. Each try and fail must be bigger than the one before it. Daffy Duck and Wiley E. Coyote are characters who often construct story and humor through this comedy cone.

Use of Classic Cartoon Character Gags

It's always good to go back to the classic cartoons for humorous ideas.

While taking a bath, Babs Bunny goes under water, and her bunny ear becomes a periscope. (*Tiny Toons* – *Bunny Daze*). This was probably borrowed from *Peanuts*: Snoopy's ears have been able to rotate like helicopter blades for decades.

Likewise, Charles Schultz borrowed from other comic strips in which the kids had lemonade stands, but put a character spin on it – Lucy opened her own stand - a psychiatric booth. "Help for five cents."

Note: Seven of the comedy cones listed above were in part derived from my first animation teacher's (Annie Montgomery) fifteen levels of humor. You'll find eight more listed under the dialogue devices in Chapter Thirteen. Thanks, Annie.

Conclusion

As illustrated in the examples above, you can mix or combine comedy cones however they work for your story. The point is to always fill the page with humor. Play with the audience expectations as you write your gags. If you have trouble thinking up gags, classic cartoons and/or black and white silent comedies are great sources of inspiration. "Borrow" from the best, updating the gag by giving it a new and fresh spin.

Exercise #53: Think back over the cartoons you've watched thus far, and/or scrutinize several new episodes, then list at least one example for each comedy cone.

This exercise will help familiarize you with comedy cones to aid you as you begin writing your teleplay in the next chapter.

Chapter Twelve
Prose

All the words on your page that aren't dialogue; sluglines or character names make up your prose. In other words, it's the words you use in describing your scene, or the action of your scene; the information you give to the animator and the story editor. In the example below:

EXT. NEIGHBORHOOD PARK – DAY (This is your slugline.)

Johnny spots a "hottie" walking her dog in the park. (This is your prose.)

Often, the prose is a neglected area in script writing, but it shouldn't be. Every word counts in your final draft. You want your whole script to be a terrific read for the story editor and the animator.

Prose Signposts

Follow these signposts to ensure your prose is on the right track.

1 Capture the tone of the cartoon tunnel for which you are writing. Be humorous, and have fun with it. Make the reader laugh here as well.

2 Keep your page balanced: don't flood your pages with ink (blocks of lengthy paragraphs). Break up the action with dialogue.

This makes your script a more appealing read as well giving it a professional appearance. If a story editor opens your script to see a page of black ink, you've given yourself away as an amateur.

Road Rule #19: LESS IS MORE! Especially in your prose (except for its humor).

3 Keep your prose between 2 to 4 lines per paragraph, and try not to exceed 6 to 8 lines per scene unless you have a long action sequence.

(If this is the case, break up prose blocks with dialogue when possible.) Make sure what you write is clear.

4   Choose action verbs over linking verbs. Load your script with strong and interesting word choices.

Don't write: Pooh *is looking* for Christopher Robbin.

Write: Pooh *searches* for Christopher Robbin.

5   Eliminate excess words. Don't describe every bit of action, only that which is necessary. For example:

INT. HAZELNUT MIDDLE SCHOOL HALLWAY – MORNING

Pepper Ann opens the door and rushes into the school hallway, late. There, she quickly scans for Principal Hickey. Relieved, Pepper Ann hurries to her classroom and opens the door. She goes inside the classroom. (35 words)

You can describe the same action just as efficiently by rewriting it this way:

INT. HAZELNUT MIDDLE SCHOOL HALLWAY – MORNING

Late, Pepper Ann sprints inside, scanning for Principal Hickey. Whew! No one in sight. She dashes into class. (18 words)

See how many words you can eliminate?

6   Be aware of language differences.

Many times, your script will be sent overseas to be animated by Korean or Japanese animation companies. In these circumstances, your script might not translate as you would expect. Be careful of using certain English expressions or euphemisms. For example, if you write that the character is crying over spilt milk, you're liking to get a picture of a character standing over a glass of spilt milk and crying – which is probably not what you had in mind.

7   Describe actions in broad and/or simple terms.

In cartoons, you can show facial expression only to certain degrees. Subtle reactions are not possible to depict in animation. Subtle doesn't apply in animation – it's broad. Here's not the place to show off your amazing vocabulary. Don't write: "Pepper Ann looks wryly at Milo." This is too subtle of a facial expression. Keep your adjectives and adverbs simple when you use them. Write, "Pepper Ann looks at Milo. No adjective needed here.

Screen Directions

In animation, you are fortunate enough to be both a writer and a director because you must explain to the animator the visual direction of the scene. You do this by using screen directions. Screen directions are just that – they tell the animation director and the animator how the frame is filled and how the action is directed. Common screen directions in animation include those listed below. They are categorized by their similar or opposite meanings:

ANGLE ON (CHARACTER OR OBJECT): Camera focuses on the character or object named.

FAVORING (CHARACTER'S NAME): angle favors the character named.

ON TWOSOME (or however many in the group): a shot which includes the number of characters specified.

(CHARACTER'S NAME) POV: Camera shoots from that character's point of view; not seeing the character, just what the character sees through their eyes.

AERIAL POV: Camera shoots far overhead.

BIRD'S EYE VIEW – Camera takes bird's point of view from above.

OVERHEAD AS CAM SWOOPS DOWN: Camera is overhead and swoops in on scene.

BACK TO: Camera returns to the shot before its preceding shot.

CAMERA SHAKES: Camera shakes to create suspense, and give the feel of more movement. Use in earthquake or similar effects scenes.

DUTCH TILT ON: Camera is turned 45 degrees so angle is tilted. Used in eerie or suspenseful situations.

ANGLE BEHIND (OBJECT): Camera shoots from behind the object named, like a boulder, tree...

THROUGH (AN OBJECT): Camera shoots through the object named, such as a magnifying glass, window, archway...

CLOSE ON: Close-Up of the character or object named.

TIGHT ON: another way of saying CLOSE ON.

DOWNSHOT ON: Camera shoots looking down on an object.

DRAMATIC UPSHOT or UPSHOT: Camera shoots looking up at the character or object.

DRAMATIC ANGLE ON: the scene is framed dramatically on a character or object.

FLASHBACK: let's the animator know the story is moving back in time.

FLASHFORWARD: let's the animator know the story is moving ahead into the future.

BACK TO PRESENT: let's the animator know story is moving to the present again. Always follows a flashback scene.

INSERT: used for extreme close ups to show a note or a clue.

LONG SHOT: camera shoots to show the distance of the scene.

OPEN CLOSE ON: use at the beginning of a scene just after its slugline.

PAN AHEAD: Camera moves to the action ahead in the scene.

PAN DOWN: Camera moves down the scene.

ON (CHARACTER'S NAME) – PANNING: Camera follows the character and his/her action.

PAN OVER: Camera moves sideways across the scene.

PAN TO: Camera pans or moves to another part of the scene.

PAN UP: Camera moves up the scene.

TRUCK IN: Camera moves in quickly on scene.

TRUCK OUT: Camera moves quickly out from scene.

SHOT WIDENS: Camera lens opens to include more of the scene.

WIDER ON SCENE: use when you want to include full scope of the action.

WIDE ON: shot shows a wide shot of the character.

WIDER TO INCLUDE (CHARACTER'S NAME): used to visually include another character in a scene.

Sometimes, you will also have certain directions at the end of your scenes and just preceding the next slugline:

DISSOLVE TO: this dissolves us into the next scene and is used most often to indicate a longer passage of time, say going from day to night, or if the following scene is the same location or setting, but occurs at a later time of day.

SMASH CUT TO: this smashes or cuts very quickly into the next scene, and is generally used for humor or suspense. It just indicates you want to cut more quickly into the next scene than normally.

CUT BACK TO: return to the previous scene.

Another important element to note when writing for animation is that you must always capitalize your SFX (sound effects). This helps the sound editor out when he's looking for the sound effects in a script. For example, a JACKHAMMER POUNDS or an owl HOOTS or a phone RINGS or a MUSIC MONTAGE.

Road Rule#20: Use a format of 52 lines per page with the 52 lines appearing between the top and bottom holes of your three-hole punched paper (brads in top and bottom holes only). This falls in the range of a .168-.172" line height using standard font "Courier New."

Exercise #54: It's time to start writing your teleplay. Regardless of your format's length, choose one of your Road Map outlines and write Act One. Use as many comedy cones as possible in your script. See the appendix for further script format.

Note: Remember, with an existing series, you must stay consistent to the show's tone and genre (Road Rule #6).

Don't read ahead before starting your script. The next few chapters will focus on more specific areas of the teleplay. In your first draft, just focus on structure and humor. If you attempt to focus on being brilliant with structure, character, dialogue, prose, humor, and format all at once, you're going to get bogged down. You'll have plenty of chances in your many rewrites to worry about the finer details.

Just start getting words on the page, and don't worry whether every word you type is a gem. Structure and humor, that's your goal with this first draft. Once you've finished your first act in the exercise above, stop writing, and continue to the next chapter.

Chapter Thirteen
Dialogue

Cartoon dialogue is different from other dialogue, and therefore can be tricky for the novice writer. In the animated world, you can't have two characters sitting or standing around chatting.

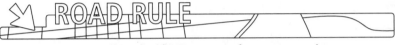

Road Rule #21: No talking heads! Keep your characters moving.

The only time this Road Rule doesn't apply, is of course, if it contradicts a rule of the serie's cartooniverse. Most likely, if you wish to write for Saturday morning cartoons, you'll always adhere to this Road Rule. Some of the prime-time (those shows on after seven o'clock central time) do not adhere to this rule for stylistic reasons, that is, it's okay in their cartooniverse to have "talking heads" in their series.

For example, *Dr. Katz* generally consists of talking heads for much of the half hour. It has a jumpy motion to give the feel of action while a patient sits on the couch pouring out his/her emotions to Dr. Katz, or while at home, Dr. Katz and Ben have their father-son chats.

Understand the rules of the particular show you want to write for and remain within those boundaries.

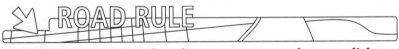

Road Rule #22: No more than three sentences per character dialogue (dialogue block).

In animated scripts, dialogue usually consists of a character speaking no more than three sentences per dialogue block (the line or several lines that make up the character's speech). Thus, don't litter your page with too much chatter. In cartoons, the characters must always be moving and involved in some kind of action. Your script will have to reflect this in both its dialogue and its prose. Again, this is a general rule. If it doesn't comply with the serie's cartooniverse, follow the rules of the cartooniverse.

Road Rule #23: Less than three speeches per page is considered not enough dialogue.

Likewise, if your animated script has less than three speeches (or dialogue blocks) per page, this is considered too sparse and is known as "dead air." Dead air means air time in which no one is talking or moving, and the camera remains on the character's reaction. If there's not enough dialogue and action to fill the air time in a script, then the director has to remain on a character for too long. Remember, timing is crucial in animation.

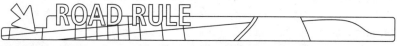

Road Rule #24: Break up speeches with movement and action.

Split a speech or dialogue block with an appropriate action. For example, as a character says one line, have him start walking, then say another line or two of dialogue. Start thinking like an animation writer, and keep those characters moving. This brings us to our next Road Rule:

Road Rule #25: Arrive late and leave early in your dialogue.

You don't want to waste time. Don't waste time having characters chat about nothing. You only have 22, 11, or 7 minutes for your story. Zoom into the dialogue as fast as you can, and keep the story moving along your story's streets.

As you study the series for which you are writing your sample episodes, listen to the rhythm of the dialogue. Dialogue is a precious tool for the writer. It can help you pull in an audience and make them laugh. It can also be the most rewarding element to write once you've mastered it.

Exercise #55: Take one of your scenes (one that has a lot of dialogue) that you wrote in your Act One and rewrite the scene with the above Road Rules in mind.

Exercise #56: Next, write:

A. Act Two and Act Three if using the 22 minute format,

B. Act Two if using the 11 minute format,

C. Continue reading if using the 7 minute format.

Dialogue Style

The type and style of dialogue you use in your episode will mainly depend on these seven factors:

1 The Character's Compass Traits and Dipsticks

2 The Character's Tics

3 The Character's Relationships

4 The Cartooniverse's Vernacular

5 The Genre

6 The Format Length

7 Age of the Target Audience

Let's look at how these factors affect the style of a serie's dialogue.

The Character's Compass Traits and Dipsticks
A character's traits and dipstick data will affect their dialogue. Obviously, if a character is an adult, he/she will speak differently than a child. The characters' dialogue on *Rugrats* will be different than that on *Dr. Katz*, especially in the content of the dialogue, although there are those subjects which are ageless:

In *Cradle Attraction – Rugrats*

> TOMMY
> She likes you? She was poking you and calling you names and pushing you down because she likes you?!

> CHUCKIE
> I know it sounds weird, but that's what she said.

> LIL
> I think she's nuts.

> PHIL
> Yeah, if I were you I'd stay out of her way. She might have rabies or something.

In an episode of *Dr. Katz*, one of his patients relays his confusion about the opposite sex:

> DR. KATZ
> Well, what is your theory about women, Larry?

> LARRY
> Ah, no matter what we do, no matter what we say, I have a feeling women always look at us like an idiot.

(mimicking his date)
"Yes, I'll have another glass of wine, you monkey. Maybe it will help me listen to your stupid stories."

Whether the character is a machine, animal, toy, human or superhuman will also affect the dialogue. Have fun with these distinctions.

In *Doug's Dog's Date – Doug*: Doug advises his pet before the big date:

DOUG

Don't do all the barking, and be home by ten.

In *Infected – Reboot*:

MEGABIT

I haven't felt this good since I was infected.

In addition, a character's compass traits will also affect his/her dialogue. In *Winnie the Pooh's Cleanliness is Next to Impossible*, Tigger stacks Christopher Robbins toys in a towering heap and asks what Pooh thinks about it.

POOH

It's very pilish.

In Pooh's vocabulary, "ish" is a popular suffix. He is also very polite, and often says, "please" and "thank you." When the monster under the bed throws back a shoe, Pooh responds:

POOH

No more shoes, please. We already have one.

Tigger's speech is often in rhyme or scattered or mixes up common expressions (turning "positively" into "posolutely" or "absolutely" into "absosurely").

In *Johnny Bravo's Johnny and the Beanstalk*, as he talks to the giant, his dry wit and sarcasm brings us such dialogue as:

JOHNNY
Except for the pain and terror, I had a great time.

The Character's Tics

A character's tic will most definitely come into play with the dialogue. Remember, some characters just have sound effects for voices or don't speak at all. You can't suddenly give them a voice with dialogue. For those who have a distinctive voice tic, like Piglet and his stutter or the Riddler's tic of speaking only in riddles means you have to cleverly incorporate this in their dialogue.

In *Peanuts*, the voice tic of the adults is, "wah, wah, wah-wah." This dialogue isn't intelligible, therefore you have to verbally communicate what is being said by how the character who is listening, responds to such dialogue.

The Characters' Relationships

The relationship between characters will always dictate dialogue style, whether they are siblings, spouses, friends, enemies or pet owner and pet, as it is a two-way street.

Eustas's dialogue with Courage is always going to be gruff and mean whereas Murial speaks to the dog kindly. (*Courage The Cowardly Dog*)

In *Rugrats*, Angelica treats the babies mischievously, and often bosses them around which her dialogue depicts.

Marcie addresses Peppermint Patty as, "Sir." (*Peanuts*)

The Cartooniverse's Vernacular

Each series will have its own vernacular sprinkled throughout the episode. Those series which are successful, will find their cartoon vernacular becomes a part of popular culture. Study the dialogue from the series you are writing to discover its particular vocabulary.

Peanuts brought the words fussbudget, crabby and blockhead to our real world conversations.

In *South Park*, the kids always swear.

In *Reboot*, the unique vocabulary of computer language graces its dialogue. You'll hear lines such as "incoming files," or a character being, "just a nano away." Or villains declaring:

MEGABITE
The core and the mainframe are mine!

Batman's cartooniverse brings us words such as "the Bat cave" and "the Batmobile."

The Flintstones have a whole stone age vocabulary. They eat Brontosaurus Burgers and live in the town of Bedrock.

If the vernacular of the cartooniverse includes that a moral or lesson is to be stated in each episode, you'll have do so.

In *Rescue Heroes, Cave -In*: the rescue team advises when in a tough spot, "Persevere, Persevere, Perseve." (Notice the use of comedy cone: rule of three)

The Genre
Genre plays an important role in the rhythm and pacing of your cartoon dialogue. An action tunnel requires humor to come mainly from the dialogue, as this genre doesn't have time to stop and create a gag sequence.

Again, in *Cave-In* as the oil flows towards the fire, one rescue member realizes that they only have a few minutes to escape, and responds, "We're toast."

Likewise, in a action-comedy tunnel, dialogue pace is particularly important because you have to link the comedy with action.

In *Night of the Cowgoyle* (*C.O.W. Boys Of Moo Mesa*) Cowlorado pursues the Bandit on horseback along a perilous cliff edge – he hurls his lasso:

COWLORADO KID
Gotcha, now, you thiefin' goldnabber!

Bandit cuts the rope just as Cowlorado yanks it. Cowlorado falls off his horse, over the cliff's edge. Hanging to the ledge, he looks at the terrain *far* below him.

COWLORADO KID

I hate it when they do that.

The Format Length

Obviously, the length of an episode dramatically affects its dialogue. You'll have to write more dialogue for a 22 minute format than for a 7 minute. In addition, in the 7 minute format, much of the dialogue will be one-liners delivered by the driver, as seen in *Johnny Bravo*.

The Target Age of the Audience

The audience a cartoon series seeks will have a definite effect on its dialogue. You must write age-appropriately, especially in content and vocabulary. In the six and under age audience, you'll have to include more exposition (information you give to an audience) so that your plot is clear. Younger audiences also enjoy funny sounding words whereas the ten to twelve audience will want to hear put-downs and comebacks.

When you write parodies, you'll have to keep the sophistication of your audience in mind as well. A younger child will get a parody of something in pop culture, but won't understand more adult literary parodies. Sometimes, you'll be writing for both kids and adults as in *The Simpsons*. Here the younger audience can laugh at the slapstick comedy while their parents can appreciate the show's wicked satire and stinging social commentary.

As you write your script, take in these seven factors in regard to the particular style of dialogue you must write.

Road Rule #26: Don't take your audience out of the script by using dialogue uncharacteristic to the series or the character!

Bart Simpson isn't going to suddenly speak politely and the characters in *South Park* won't be adding, "ish" to their words as Pooh does. Mind the rules of the cartooniverse.

So how do you write good dialogue that's funny? Through practice and through the use of dialogue devices.

Dialogue Devices

These devices can make any of your script dialogue read more interestingly and more humorously.

1 Alliterations

2 Breaks The Fourth Wall

3 Character Asks A Question

4 Characters Answers With A Question

5 Character Gives Advice

6 Character Gives Order

7 Character Makes Observation

8 Character Misinterprets Conversation

9 Character Misinterprets Scene

10 Character Talks To Him/herself

11 Clichés

12 Comebacks

13 Complaints

14 Interrupt the character

15 Interrupt the scene

16 Lists

17 Manuals

18 Narrator

19 Puns

20 Put-Downs

21 Repeat dialogue

22 Rhyme Scheme

23 Segues

24 Show opposite of what character says

25 Signature Lines

26 Use of Visual Aids

27 Verbal Parody

28 Verbal Toppers

29 Words Which Sound Funny

Alliterations

Alliteration is a repetition of initial sounds in adjacent words or syllables.

In *Bad Neighbor Beetlejuice*, Ginger the spider is dancing when suddenly a big burly cop (with a voice parody of Jack Webb from *DRAGNET*) bursts in:

> COP
>
> Excuse me, Ma'am. Freeze!
>
> (Order)

> GINGER
>
> (screams)

> COP
>
> You're under arrest, you toe-tapping terrorist.
>
> (Alliteration & Rhyme Scheme)

GINGER

…I wouldn't hurt a fly.

(Cliché)

He glances over to her spider web - there's dozens of flies trapped.

COP

Uh, huh. Let's go, twinkle toes.

(Alliteration & Rhyme scheme)

Breaks The Fourth Wall
When a character turns and speaks directly into the camera, that is known as breaking the fourth wall, like the characters Beetlejuice, Johnny Bravo, and Garfield.

In *G.I.R.L. Squad – Dexter's Laboratory*, the girls go about "gathering" evidence. One of the girl detectives snatches up a cat, then turns to the camera and says:

LEE LEE

He could be a cat burglar.

Character Asks A Question
Here, you build the humor off a question.

In *Rugrats – The Word of the Day*, the babies ponder on how words can be "bad."

CHUCKIE

How can a word be bad?

TOMMY

I guess a bad word is a word people don't want to hear.

PHIL

Then I know a really bad word - bath!

Characters Answers With A Question

Here, you build your humor from the character's response, using a question.

In *Ace In Space – Ace Ventura Pet Detective*, Ace battles Padar (parody of Darth Vadar) and two storm troopers.

PADAR

Prepare to meet your doom.

ACE

Sorry, I'm not properly dressed for doom, could ya come back later?

Character Gives Advice

In *Truth or Scare – Sabrina*, Uncle Quigley takes the kids on a camping trip. Along the hiking trail, he advises:

UNCLE QUIGLEY

Keep an eye out for snakes.

- As he steps on a snake who reacts crumpled (Gag). Unaware, Uncle Quigley continues hiking.

UNCLE QUIGLEY

I hate snakes.

The snake reacts, sticking out its forked tongue (Topper).

Character Gives Order

In *Shirley The Medium – Courage The Cowardly Dog*, Eustas tries to contact, via a crystal ball and a medium, his dead brother to find out where his brother hid the key to the cash box. Instead, his wife Muriel's, dead relative starts speaking, and the two women discuss a jam recipe so Eustas interrupts:

EUSTAS

Hang up! You're tying up the line.

In *A Boy and His Bird - Johnny Bravo* tries to pick up a woman walking her poodle in the park.

JOHNNY

Hey, Baby, lose the pooch. I'm all the puppy love you need.

In *The Legend of Skull Duggery – C.O.W. Boys Of Moo Mesa*, the Sheriff's two lackeys hopes to impress their boss and get a promotion, dash when the ghost sends them flying out of the mine in a mine car.

BOOT HILL

Promotion, my Aunt Sally.

SADDLE SORE

Don't tell nobody about this, including me!

Character Makes Observation

In *Ape Is Enough – Johnny Bravo*, Johnny takes note of the cave as the Ape waves him around:

JOHNNY

I like your place, the dirt really sets off the mildew.

Character Misinterprets Conversation

Using this device can not only add humor, but further fuel your plot and build plot tension as the audience waits for the misinterpretation to be realized.

In *Word of the Day – Rugrats*, Angelica overhears Miss Carol saying the new fun phrase, only Miss Carol's being sarcastic, and the phrase is a "bad" word. Now the audience waits for Angelica to say that word on live television, which she does in the climax.

Character Misinterprets Scene

In *Ape is Enough – Johnny Bravo*, lands on the island as hostile natives emerge from the jungle, waving their spears at him.

Johnny Bravo

It's an interpretive dance troupe.

Character Talks To Himself

This can be used to provide another bit of exposition or for humor. Often characters mumble to themselves in complaint. The classic characters Yosemite Sam and Daffy Duck often use this dialogue device.

Clichés

Clichés are phrases which we have heard so much they have become trite. Whereas in screenplays, we moan if we hear a cliché, in cartoons, you can put a new twist on them and get a laugh.

In *Trouble on Arlia – Dragon Ball Z*, the cliché is used with a visual image to create the joke. As Vegeta blows up a planet:

NAPPA

There goes the neighborhood.

In *Hare Conditioned*, the cliché "Another day, another dollar" becomes:

BUGS

Another day, another carrot.

In an episode of *Space Ghost*, the cliché, "I'm your man," plays as a pun for Zorac (a praying mantis):

ZORAC

They said they needed a key boardist, and I said, "I'm your man-tis."

Comebacks

A comeback is a sarcastic or humorous response by one character to another.

After *Pepper Ann's* humiliating attempt to dive from the high board in *Have You Ever Been Unsupervised*, she tries to shrug off her embarrassment, but Milo can't resist a comeback:

PEPPER ANN

In fact, I thought I handled myself with a lot of grace and dignity.

MILO

Was that before or after you hurled in the fire truck?

Complaints

Complaints are used often as villain disparagement or to help make the character kid relatable.

In "Have You Ever Been Unsupervised," Pepper Ann worries about having to play "spin the bottle" at the party. She hopes her mother won't allow her to go because it is going to be unsupervised. But her mother surprises her by letting her.

PEPPER ANN

First, our party's unsupervised, and now my own mother decides to trust me.

In *Summer Sucks – South Park*, Cartman is trying to be optimistic about having to take swimming lessons with the first graders, while his friends discuss how awful it will be.

CARTMAN

I'm trying to make the best of a bad situation - I don't need to hear crap from a bunch of hippie freaks living in denial.

Interrupt the character

In *I Love Lisa – The Simpsons*, Lisa seeks advice (device #5) on how to let Ralph down gently. As Marge starts to answer, Homer walks in, overhearing Lisa's request:

MARGE

Well, honey…

HOMER

Let me handle this Marge, I've heard them all: "I like you as a friend," "I think we should see other people," "I don't speak English…"

LISA

I get the idea.

HOMER
"I'm married to the sea," "I don't want to kill you, but I will."

You can and should have toppers in your lines of dialogue just as you have in your gags. Here, the line, "I don't want to kill you, but I will," is the Topper to this dialogue sequence.

Interrupt the scene
Here, something or someone interrupts the scene.

In Homer Simpson in *Kidney Trouble*' – *The Simpsons*, while at the hospital, the scene is interrupted repeatedly by a VO from the intercom:

INTERCOM (VO)
Doc Martins to pediatry.
(Parody - brand name spin)

INTERCOM (VO)
Doctor Bombay, come right away.
(Parody)

Lists
Having a character read from a list is another way to provide a touch of humor to a scene. Or just listing within the story as a narrator, works as well.

In *Annoying Things*, Garfield lists "A Host of Annoying Things" on his TV show as we see visuals referenced by the dialogue:

GARFIELD
Door to door alligator salesmen...The kid who reminds the Teacher that she forgot to assign homework...Cards falling from magazines...

Manuals
Here, a character uses a manual to help him in his situation. You can really get mileage out of this mechanism.

In *City on the...*, *South Park* updates the manual device by making it a video manual. As the school bus perilously teeters on the edge of a cliff, the Bus Driver pops in the video to see what to do. It states no matter what the situation, the kids are safer on the bus – "Don't let them leave the bus!" Then it instructs the Bus Driver to tell the kids they must not get off the bus or they'll be eaten by, "a big, black, hairy monster." Of course, when one kid does finally get off the bus, he is eaten by a big, black, hairy spider.

In *Night of the Ed! – Cow & Chicken*, Cow reads the instructions from his pet manual:

COW

Oh, look, what to do if your jackal gets loose.

CHICKEN

What's it say?

COW

Step One: Panic.

CHICKEN

I'm there. Step Two?

COW

Step Two: There is no Step Two.

Narrator

On screen narration is when a character talks to the audience in this manner: the character's voice over (VO) is heard over various visuals. The character may or may not be in the scene as he talks, although if s/he is in the scene s/he *isn't* looking into the camera and talking (Breaking the 4th wall).

This humor technique can set a tone, give us insight into the driver, and also reveal exposition. Narration can play throughout the cartoon or serve as book ends (used only at the beginning and the end of the cartoon). When using this device, you will need to type "VO" which stands for "Voice Over" after the character's name in the dialogue like this:

BUGS BUNNY (VO)

Narration combined with flashbacks is a great way to reveal exposition. By flashing back, the audience gets to experience the *emotion and humor* of the scene, rather than just the *telling* of it. Parodying also combines well this device.

Narration is a rule of *Doug's* cartooniverse. In *Doug's Dog's Date*, his narration style is that of a 1940's detective as he trails Pork Chop. The visuals reflect what's being said. The last visual reveals Patty in the park, the girl Doug has a crush on:

DOUG (VO)

...11:45 a.m. Trailed Pork Chop all morning: listens to sappy music, mopes a lot, refused to chase a car. Tailing my dog was becoming an obsession. Nothing was going to keep me from getting to the bottom of this...That is, until she showed up...

Using a narrator is fun and can quickly get you into cartoon dialogue mode. Juxtaposing the dialogue against the factual visuals can add humor as well.

Puns

Cartoons thrive on puns which are simply the humorous use of a word in a way that suggests two or more interpretations.

In *Beetlejuice – Bad Neighbor Beetlejuice*, he wakes up and his stomach literally becomes a mouth (Physical feat) complaining:

STOMACH

I'm hungry.

Beetlejuice looks at the camera (Breaking 4th wall).

Beetlejuice

Upset stomach.

Sebastian the crab goes off to see Ariel's father (*The Little Mermaid – The Great Sebastian*). His parting words:

SEBASTIAN
I hope the king is in a good mood today. He can be crabbier than me.

Put-Downs

A put-down is a bit like name calling, or a type of insult. This device generally serves the action or action comedy tunnels as there is little or no time for gag sequences. You'll find this device, however, in all the genres.

Gem, a Sunday driver type, keeps calling Sabrina Smellman instead of her real name, Spellman. (*Sabrina – Truth or Scare*)

In *Courage The Cowardly Dog*, Eustas is always scolding, *Stupid Dog*.

In "A Boy and His Bird" – *Johnny Bravo*, Johnny chases after a squirrel who escapes him:

JOHNNY
You win this round, my fluffy nemesis.

Repeat dialogue

You can repeat a line of dialogue either in the same scene or throughout the story, using it to payoff somewhere in the script.

In *Ape Is Enough – Johnny Bravo*, as the boat travels across the water we hear:

JOHNNY
Are we there yet?

POP
No.

JOHNNY
Are we there yet?

POP
No!

JOHNNY

Are we there yet?

Notice the magic number of three (comedy cone 16) The line is repeated 3 times for humor.

Rhyme Scheme

This is a very popular device, especially when characters are given a clue. It helps "humorize" the exposition of the clue.

Tigger sings in a rhyme scheme, illustrating how to put away the toys by stuffing them under the bed. (*Adventures of Winnie the Pooh – Cleanliness is Next to Impossible*)

TIGGER

...The closet's too dark, and the box is too small, and the drawer they're no fun at all. This is posolutely the perfect spot. It is where it is, and it's not where it's not.

In *Johnny and the Beanstalk*, Johnny scoffs at the giant:

JOHNNY

Is that all you got, Sasquatch?

Segues

A segue is a shift into the next scene or next act. You can have many different kinds of segue, though quite often they will be in the form of an declaration, order, question or threat:

In *G.I.R.L. Squad*, Dee Dee needs help from Dexter. The scene's last line is:

DEE DEE

There's only one man who can help us now.

The scene SMASH CUTS to Dexter in his laboratory.

Show opposite of what character says

A character can say one thing to prove his point, while a visual image contrasts his dialogue for humor.

Having forgotten to get Marge a Valentine's present, Homer tries to get himself out of trouble by arguing that no one makes a fuss over Valentine's Day. Suddenly, the family hears singing. Out their window, they see Flanders serenading his wife. Homer moans. (*The Simpsons – I Love Lisa*)

Signature Lines

In the animated world, characters often use certain catch phrases, which when used repeatedly by only that character, comes to be known as a "signature" line. When an audience here's this line, they immediately think of the character to which it belongs.

BART SIMPSON

Aye Carramba!

Johnny Bravo

Yeah, whatever.

CARTMAN

Screw you guys, I'm going home.

Classic signature lines include:

FRED FLINTSTONE

Yabba Dabba Do.

YOGI BEAR

Hey, hey, hey.

BUGS BUNNY

Eh, what's up, Doc?

Use of Visual Aids

Slides shows and home movies can add visual humor while also providing exposition and help set up the story.

McBark shows slides over a monotone speech. (*Dexter's Laboratory – G.I.R.L. Squad*)

Nigel shows his family a home movie of when he first met Rebecca, the elephant. (*The Thornberry's – Forget Me Not*)

Verbal Parody
A verbal parody is a comical or satirical *verbal* imitation of someone or something.

In "Moving Away" – *Rugrats*, Angelica parodies Sally Field's famous Academy Award acceptance speech when the babies tell her they will miss her:

                    ANGELICA
You like me, you really like me!

In *I Love Lisa – Rugrats*, during the President's Play, Bart who plays John Wilkes Booth, points his gun at Lincoln (Milhouse) and parodies The Terminator:

                    BART
Hasta la vista, baby!

Ace Ventura Pet Detective's Ace In Space parodies a classic cartoon, *Scooby Doo*:

                    ACE
Well, well, let's see who our mystery guest is…"

He yanks off Padar's mask and cape to reveal a Trekky.

                    PADAR
Dang! I would have gotten away with it too if it hadn't been for you, you meddling pet detective.

Verbal Toppers
Just as in the comedy cones, you can have Toppers in your dialogue as well.

During their "spin the bottle" game, the bottle spins to Pepper Ann and she leaps up, proclaiming she isn't ready for this grown up game. (*Pepper Ann – Have You Ever Been Unsupervised?*)

PEPPER ANN
...I'm lame, and I'm proud.

Her best friend looks at her.

NICKY
Ah, Pepper Ann? It's pointing at me.

Pepper looks down to see the bottle points at Nicky.

Words Which Sound Funny
The younger audience love funny sounding words so use this device frequently when writing to the six and under audience.

In *How Much is that Rabbit in the Window? – Winnie The Pooh*, the group tries to catch lightning bugs called "flutterflies."

Conclusion

As illustrated from all the examples above, you can combine dialogue devices with each other, and with comedy cones to enhance the humor in your dialogue. Get familiar with spotting these devices as you study cartoons. It takes time and experience to learn to write dialogue well. By applying these devices, you can make your dialogue an enjoyable read.

Dialogue Signposts

To test dialogue as you write, check it against these signposts:

1 Is it revealing backstory, information on, or the personality of a character?

2 Is it giving the audience more information of your plot or subplot?

3 Does it have to be said in dialogue, or would it play better as a visual gag?

4 Is the line of dialogue really necessary, or can it be eliminated altogether?

Examine each line, especially the first and last lines of dialogue in a scene. Can you cut them, and zoom right into the scene? Most likely, the answer is yes. Often, you'll find your characters are speaking more like *real* people than *reel* people when you begin and end a scene.

Exercise #57: Pick a scene from your script with the longest amount of dialogue. Go through this scene, reviewing ONLY the dialogue. If any piece of dialogue does not correctly follow one of the signposts, dump it! It's littering your page. Rewrite lines using any of the dialogue devices that will make your dialogue stronger. Once you've rewritten the dialogue, reread your scene. Listen to how much tighter it sounds, and how your pacing has improved.

Note: Don't start rewriting the whole script yet, just this one scene. The rewrite comes in a later chapter.

With your new knowledge of dialogue, it's time to begin your second teleplay.

Exercise #58: Regardless of your format length, take your 2nd Road Map outline, and write Act One. Include the dialogue devices discussed in this chapter.

Note: Don't worry about making your dialogue perfect. This is just to help familiarize you with dialogue devices. As with your first script, the first draft is about getting the plot and gags secured on the page. Everything else, you can rework in the rewrites.

Chapter Fourteen
The Scene

A scene is one of the story elements used to write a script. You create a new scene each time you switch location (even if the next scene is just in the next room) or time of day (even if the next scene is just a few minutes later). The length of a scene in animation may vary from 1/8 of a page to 3 pages, that is, from a few short seconds to a minute and a half. The shorter the script's length, the shorter your scenes will be on average. Thus, in animation writing, movement is crucial.

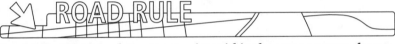

Road Rule #27: Keep characters moving within the scene or move them to another scene!

Too long a scene without enough gags or action could make for a fidgety audience, or worse, one that switches channels.

In the individual scene, the same rules apply as in the overall plot construction. Each scene has a beginning, middle, end, and each has an incline (stakes rising) which grows steeper in each individual street (scene).

For example, let's pick some scenes from our example episodes:

(*The Simpsons – I Love Lisa*) In the beginning of the classroom scene: Teacher tells everyone to exchange Valentines. Lisa notices no one gives Ralph a card.

The middle of the scene: Lisa sympathetically makes a Valentine card for Ralph and gives it to him (incline rising).

In the end of the scene: Ralph reads it excitedly, and thinks Lisa likes him. Now, he's got a crush on her (incline peaked).

(*Rugrats – The Word of the Day*) In the episode's opening, the beginning of the scene: Angelica watches Miss Carol's show. Tommy joins her.

The middle of the scene: Angelica explains to Tommy that they are about to draw names for a new helper. She waits, wanting desperately to be Miss Carol's helper (incline rising as now there is something at stake in the scene).

In the end of the scene: Names are drawn, and Angelica's name is one of them. Angelica shrieks excitedly – she gets to audition to be the new helper (incline peaked).

(*Dexter's Laboratory – G.I.R.L. Squad*) in the beginning of the scene: Dee Dee asks for her brother's help.

The middle of the scene: Dexter shows the girls various James Bond devices for catching criminals (incline rising).

In the end of the scene: Dexter dumps the girls from his laboratory (incline peaked).

Although each of the above examples is from different genres and formats, each scene is constructed in the same way: with a beginning, a middle and an end.

As you construct your plot, keep in mind:

Road Rule#28: Arrive late and leave early in your scenes.

Just as in your dialogue, you want to enter a scene at the last possible minute and leave it as soon as you can. In addition, when writing your scene, remember:

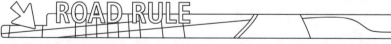

Road Rule #29: Your character must leave each scene needing more and/or knowing more than when he entered it!

As you construct your scenes, think about them in terms of telling their own mini-story. When your character enters the scene you are writing, that's the most important scene to him/her. Remember, your characters don't know what's coming next, so don't write them as if they do.

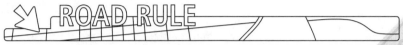

Road Rule #30: Write the unexpected scene. Keep surprising the audience (and your driver) in a believable manner.

Slippery When Wet – The Oblique Scene

What makes a scene unique? Chances are whatever you think of first, that's what every other writer's going to think of too. Dig down deep for your ideas. As you write a scene, think of at least three or four ways to approach that scene, then discard the first three because by your fourth attempt, you've probably come up with something fresh. You want to write the *oblique* scene, not the *obvious* scene. Slide your driver in an unexpected direction. In comedy, it's the unexpected that tickles our funny bone and makes us laugh.

The best way to achieve writing a unique scene is to take a scene familiar to an audience and put a spin on it – slide it in a direction they aren't expecting. When you research cartoons, pay attention to what scenes catch you unexpectedly and cause you to laugh aloud. Take note, because this is what you want to do in your own scripts to create comedy (and sometimes, to create suspense).

A coyote goes to sit on the edge of a cliff in the lonely, moonlit night. He opens his mouth to howl mournfully – suddenly we hear another character singing horribly. Chagrined, the coyote sighs and slumps off without a sound. This takes a familiar western scene and spins it for an unexpected laugh. (*Winnetoons* - pilot)

When the parents decide to go out for the evening, but have no babysitter, one would expect them to let Chicken babysit as he is the older sibling, but the parents decide by letting the biggest of their

---

children babysit, which is Cow. The humor is milked (pardon the pun) from Cow's enthusiasm for the job. (*Cow & Chicken – The Baby Sitter*)

Allow me to digress once more to a film example because it is the quintessential example of taking a familiar scene the audiences has viewed dozens of time and sliding it into a surprise direction for a huge laugh:

Indiana Jones tries to escape the market place, but a man looms ahead slicing the air impressively with his swords. The audience is pumped for (and expects) a martial arts battle – How is Indiana going to get out of this one? Indiana frowns; it's been a tough day. He takes out his pistol and shoots the guy. It's a brilliant and unexpected spin, and the audience roars with laughter. (*Raiders of the Lost Ark*)

Note: This is how a writer should write the oblique scene. Unfortunately, this wasn't a scene written in the script. It came about when Harrison Ford showed up for an eight hour day of stunt work. Ford, however, had the flu, and only had one hour of work in him. Thus, the scene was improvised so Ford could go to his hotel and recuperate.

Don't count on serendipity to make your scenes memorable ones. Come at the scene from an unlikely direction. As a writer, it's your job to envision scenes like these. This is how you create comedy. Push yourself to write original scenes, for each and every street must keep the viewer riding along with your driver.

During the outline process, your focus is first on plot, but when writing a scene, focus on the characters and the gags. Make your driver smash into a scene head-on by hurling something emotional at him, or something unexpected. Your job as the writer is to make your driver's life difficult for the next 44 or 22 or 14 pages. Take that job very seriously – and very humorously.

Exercise #59: Choose the longest scene you wrote in Act One of your second teleplay. Rewrite it from three different approaches using the Road Rules in this chapter. Don't edit any of your ideas as you write, just write whatever comes to mind. Number each attempt.

Once you've written these three different versions (plus your original draft) *take a two day Pit Stop.* DO NOT do the exercise below until you have "refueled" your imagination. Again, I can't stress enough the importance of coming at your work with "fresh" eyes.

Exercise #60: Now that you've had several days to clear your mind, read your four scene attempts. Which one reads the best? Which version sounds the most funny and fresh? Most likely, the draft you choose won't be your first attempt. Insert the scene you choose into your teleplay before moving to the next exercise.

Exercise #61: Knowing each scene has its own beginning, middle, and end, attempt to write the oblique scene as you continue your second teleplay. If you are writing for:

A. The 22 minute format: write Acts Two & Three,

B. The 11 minute format: write Act Two,

C. The 7 minute format: continue to the paragraph below.

Exercise #62: Once you've finished your second script, take a two week Pit Stop!

Clear your mind. You want to be able to have an objective view of your work before reading through it. You can only obtain this by taking a significant time away from your teleplays. In this way, your mistakes will leap off the page at you. If you rush to the next chapter, I promise you, you won't be half as productive.

Chapter Fifteen
Broadcast Guidelines

Every broadcaster (CBS, NBC, ABC, FOX, Nickelodeon…) has it's own set of stringent guidelines for what is acceptable to them to broadcast. These guidelines exist to protect them against law suits and to protect their audiences as well. As an animation writer, most likely, your target audience is children. You have a responsibility to that audience. Kids love to mimic, especially their animated heroes, so Drive Safely. It's better to discard a joke or visual gag than write one which could end up harmful to a child who might imitate it. Anyway, your script won't be aired until it's met the rules and guidelines of the Broadcaster.

Gags or jokes you could write for a FOX or Comedy Channel series most likely wouldn't be allowed in a Disney animation series. You can get a really good idea of what you can or cannot write by studying the rules of the serie's cartooniverse for which you are writing. For the most part, however, use your common sense. You can be almost certain you WON'T be allowed to include the situations below in any cartoon produced currently.

Safety Checklist

1 No guns pointing at people, especially their heads.

This rule is especially important for obvious reasons. You can, however, use "fantasy guns." For example, a gun that doesn't look anything like a realistic gun. Guns which "vaporize" or turn a villain into ice, are okay to use. Even a "fantasy gun" cannot be aimed at a character's head.

2 No knives at any character's throat.

3 No ropes or binding around anyone's neck.

Thus bolos and nooses are a no-no. Don't have a character grab another character by the neck or choke another character either in a scene.

4 No deliberate hitting of face or head, especially with objects such as hammers.

You can allow an *anvil* to fall on a character as in the classic cartoons. Why? Because, most likely no kid has access to an anvil nor could he/she lift it to repeat the act if he/she did.

5 *Never* put any character in an oven, washing machine, dryer, refrigerator, microwave, food processor...

6 No ingestion of foreign or magical potions.

7 No poking fingers in the eyes, or spraying of anything in the eyes.

8 No lead character should intentionally hurt another character.

9 No torturing or teasing of animals.

Other Considerations

Use of swearing, name calling (such as idiot, moron, stupid) and potty humor are not acceptable on some cartoons. Likewise, certain broadcasters avoid tales of possession and black magic. Check the rules of your cartooniverse to see if any of these are allowed if you want to use them in your script.

In addition, you'll need to be PC (politically correct) in your scripts. This means that for every ethnic bad guy, you must have an ethnic good guy of the same race or culture so as to show a balance. This applies especially if you are creating your own series. Make sure to integrate your characters in a culturally and ethnically diverse group.

Legal Checklist

For legal reasons

1 Never have the announcer say, "We interrupt this program for an emergency broadcast..."

   This follows the "War of the Worlds" lesson in which thousands of people believed the United States was actually being attacked by Martians.

   Legally, you cannot do this due to FCC Broadcasting Standards.

2 Do not use names that are commercially identifiable.

   It's okay to make it a parody, just not a product placement (places products within a television show or film for advertising purposes). For example, perhaps Daffy eats "Ducky Charms" instead of "Lucky Charms" cereal.

3 If there's a song you need, use music which is public domain.

   You may be surprised to learn "Happy Birthday" is a copyrighted song, so don't use it. Use "For he's a jolly good fellow" or something similar instead.

Exercise #63: Go through your two teleplays, using the criteria above and make any necessary changes for your script. Remember, if it's allowed in the particular cartooniverse you are writing for, go ahead and use it.

You want to get rid of any unacceptable gag or illegal faction here so you can concentrate only on the creative issues in the following chapter.

Now that you've made your teleplays broadcaster-acceptable, it's time to focus on the rewrite.

Chapter Sixteen
The Rewrite

Congratulations! You've finished two animated scripts. Now it's time to clean up your streets.

Road Rule #31: REWRITE! REWRITE & REWRITE!

You want to drive through each of your teleplays using the checklists listed. Go drive through only one checklist at a time. DO NOT attempt to check your scripts scene by scene using all the checklists at once. You need to approach it from an overall view, and then move inward. Be sure to take an appropriate Pit Stop between each "drive" through your teleplay. You don't want to start a new pass when you're tired of your script. (And you will get tired of it – that's when you know it's time for a Pit Stop.)

Structure Checklist

If you diligently structured your Road Map, your plot should be fine. Still, it's good to make sure your characters didn't drive off the road as you were writing. You want to fix any crumbling streets in this first rewrite.

Exercise #64: Go through your first teleplay, using the checklist below, and scrutinize your structure. Examine only your plot for now.

1 If any two scenes accomplish exactly the same thing, cut one, no matter how funny or brilliant it may be – lose it!

2 Have you written your scenes so that each city block has its own beginning, middle, and end? Does each block have an incline (jeopardy or what's at stake) which is rising?

3 Have you created enough falling rocks (appropriate to its cartooniverse and cartoon tunnel) for your driver within each city block?

4 Are your Tow-Away, Green Light, U-Turn, On Ramp & No Outlet Ramps (if applicable) strong enough to speed your story into their respective acts?

Checklist for Your Characters

Now that you have passed through your teleplay and inspected it for structure, it's time to do the same with your characters.

Exercise #65: Go through your first teleplay, using the checklist below, and examine your characters, and ONLY your characters.

1 Does your driver appear on the first page of your script and stop on the last page? He's/ She's who the audience is expecting so make sure the driver (or maybe the villain in a 22 minute format) starts off the story on page 1.

2 Is your driver consistent to his/her cartooniverse, dipstick, true North and character compass?

3 Are your supporting characters, sidekicks, and villains consistent?

4 If you created your own characters, are they unique and funny? Are they relatable to your audience?

5 When you first introduced new characters (if applicable) did you make their tags whimsical and unique?

6 If applicable, does the character embody the moral or lesson learned in the outcome of the story?

7 Have you created a worthy adversary for your driver? Does your antagonist have a forceful goal and emotional need which is in direct conflict with your driver's goal and/or need?

Checklist for Your Scenes

Do not proceed unless you've taken a few days off during a Pit Stop. Then, go on and inspect your individual scenes.

Exercise #66: Go through your first teleplay, using the checklist below, and evaluate scene by scene.

1 Does each scene have its own beginning, middle, and end? Is it rising as well?

2 Have you written the oblique/unexpected scene, or a scene the audience has experienced many times?

3 Is your character leaving each scene, knowing more than when he/she entered it?

4 Do you arrive late and leave early in each of your scenes?

5 Are your characters moving within the scene, or do you have talking heads?

6 Have you grabbed your reader on page one?

Checklist for Your Dialogue

Have you taken an appropriate Pit Stop? You want to have refueled your imagination before taking on the dialogue.

Exercise #67: Go through your first teleplay, using the checklist on p. 150 and examine your characters dialogue, and ONLY your characters dialogue.

1 Are you arriving late and leaving early in your dialogue?

As you rewrite your script, go through the dialogue and find the one line which is the fuel (essence) of the scene, and highlight it. Then go back through the scene and toss as many lines before and after that line as you can.

A. This is also a great place to look for repeating lines which don't need to be repeated:

For example. "I can't believe you did that. What were you thinking?"

You don't need both of these lines, one does the job.

2 Does the dialogue vary or does it all sound like the same character?

Go through your teleplay reading ONLY one character's dialogue at a time. This illuminates inconsistencies in the character's dialogue and speech patterns. Repeat this process with each character in your script, checking each line against these seven checkpoints:

A. Is it consistent for your character compass traits and dipstick?

B. If applicable, is it consistent with the character's tic?

C. Is it consistent with the character's relationship to whom he/she is speaking to?

D. Is it consistent with the cartooniverse's vernacular?

E. Is it in keeping with the style of your genre?

F. Is it appropriate for the length of your format?

G. Is it age-appropriate for your target audience?

Now, examine the dialogue as a whole:

3 Do you need to jazz up your dialogue in the scene by using some of the dialogue devices discussed in Chapter 13?

4 Does each line of dialogue fulfill at least one of the dialogue signposts listed in Chapter 13? Check to make sure it does.

5 If a character has a signature line, have you used it? (Don't over use it.)

6 When you enter a scene (except for action sequences) are you getting to the dialogue as quickly as possible?

7 Do you have more than three lines per block of character dialogue? If so (unless okay with the cartooniverse rules) then delete dialogue.

8 Do you have less than three blocks of dialogue per page? Do you have "talking heads" when you shouldn't have? If you do, you'll need to add dialogue.

9 Is it kid-relatable?

10 Are you most likely within the broadcaster's guidelines of what is appropriate dialogue for their cartoon show?

11 If it is a comedic line, is it *funny*?!

Checklist for Humor

After you've taken a well-earned Pit Stop from the exercise above, then continue. You're script is getting stronger with each rewrite. Now it's down to the fine-tuning.

Exercise #68: Go through your first teleplay, using the checklist below, and really hone your gags and jokes. Polish your comedy cones.

1 Is the comedy cone consistent with the rules of its cartooniverse & genre?

2 Is it consistent with the characters?

3 Do you need to add more comedy cones?

4 Are your visual gags *funny*?!

5 Does each Topper, truly top the last gag?

6 Does your comedy play to the scene and move the story forward?

Checklist for Your Prose

Congratulations! It's time for that last polish.

Exercise #69: Go through your first teleplay, and follow the checklist for your prose.

1 Are you choosing action verbs and other strong word choices?

2 Have you eliminated all excess words?

3 Are you describing action that isn't necessary to describe? If yes, eliminate it.

4 Is the action you are describing clear to the reader?

5 Have you included screen directions in the appropriate places?

6 Is your action broken up so that it doesn't look as if you've flooded your page with ink?

7 Do you have humor in your prose?

8 Have you captured the genre's tone in your prose?

9 Have you capitalized all SFX (sound effects) in your script?

10 Have you described any reactions which are too subtle for an animator to draw? If so, eliminate them.

11 Are there any English expressions or euphemisms which might not translate as you intend them to a foreign speaking animator?

That's it! You did it! You survived the rewrite process. Be proud of your hard work; your script reflects all your efforts. Hopefully, it will pay off – literally.

Exercise #70: Take a much needed Pit Stop before starting this process all over for your second teleplay.

Exercise #71: Once you're ready to start the next rewrite, repeat exercises 63-68 for your 2nd teleplay.

Remember, make sure your first five pages read brilliantly!

Everybody's A Critic

This is a good thing because it's time to hand your scripts out to trusted friends to read. Choose those friends who are brave enough to tell you what works and what doesn't work in your teleplays, what's funny and what isn't. Once you get their notes, take another Pit Stop. Give yourself a few days before polishing your scripts for the final time. You want to absorb what's been said by your reviewers. The more time away from your scripts, the more objectively you can approach your polish. You might not use all the notes you get, but if you consistently get the same note on a certain area of your script, odds are, your friends are right in their assessment.

Exercise #72: Polish your first teleplay regarding the comments you received. Then polish your second script.

Okay, now it's time to get your script out into the world of animation so all your hard work can hopefully pay off.

Chapter Seventeen
The Process

It's time to enter into the world of the animation industry. In this world, there is a development process every animation writer participates in when writing on freelance assignment. Strut your humor throughout each and every speed bump in the process, because until you get to script, your story can be dumped along the way. Guiding you through this process, is the story editor.

The Story Editor

This is the person who controls most of the stories, and the person to whom you will pitch your ideas. The story editor(s) will be the buffer between you and the studio, producer and broadcaster. They are the writers who have most likely created the series. Generally, they write the first six episodes of the series themselves, due to tight production schedules. This can leave up to seven episodes to be freelanced (assigned to other writers who are paid on a contract basis). The exceptions to this are prime time animation series like *The Simpsons* and *Dr. Katz* which have staff writers, although there are freelance assignments in prime time as well.

Note: If you pitch to a prime time series, you probably will pitch to the producers of the show whereas if you pitch to daytime series, you'll be pitching to story editors.

Throughout the animation writing process, story editors will help you with the premise, the treatment, the beat outline, and the script, providing you are approved to continue through each phase. The story editors go through the story, scene by scene, helping you plot your story and helping you create gags for your story. They are your "Triple AAA" team along your creative highway, pointing out any flaws in your story and assisting you in finding solutions.

Okay, so you've written, rewritten, and rewritten your teleplays. Once they are in the best possible shape, send them to as many story editors as you can find who will read your sample scripts. First, however, you'll have to send a query letter to get permission to submit your script.

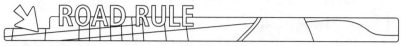

Road Rule #32: Never send your script to a company without first getting permission!

You can get a contact name from the production company list in Variety's Special Animation Issue which comes out every February. From there, you can ask for the story editor's number + address. You can also get the story editor's name and the distribution company's name (DIC, Disney, Hanna Barbara…) from the cartoon's credits. Contact the studio that produces the series in which you are interested, and get the story editor's number + address.

In your query letter, include as succinctly as possible:

1 That you are an animation writer seeking a freelance assignment. That you have two sample scripts to show from other series which are in the same cartoon genre as theirs.

2 List any previous writing positions, awards, and/or nominations you have acquired (even if it's not in the animation area). You want to prove you are marketable as a writer.

3 Thank the person for his/her time in considering your script.

It's okay to mass solicit (sending out multiple query letters) although only query about three at a time, then wait before sending out three more.

Hopefully, you'll receive positive responses, although it might even be several weeks or even a month before you receive a reply. Keep sending out query letters or making cold calls until you find someone who will read your script.

Exercise #73: Send out 6 query letters or make 6 cold calls to story editors, asking to pitch for a freelance assignment. Repeat this exercise until you have a freelance assignment.

Keep a list of to whom and when you sent letters or made calls.

Note: The best time to reach story editors is during their down time which is roughly from August through January (for day time cartoons). It's more difficult for them to read sample scripts during their production time, but they will. Just be more patient during these months.

The Script Submission

Okay, you've received permission to submit your script, sent it off, and now it's in the story editor's hands. As he/she reads your teleplay, you will be judged on how well you know the rules of the series and of animation. Your story structure, characters, dialogue, gags, and style will be evaluated. If you haven't received a response in three weeks of sending your script, then call them. Don't pester, but do be persistent. They are extremely busy, and might have forgotten your script.

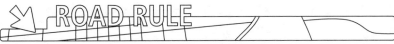

Road Rule #33: Don't take rejection personally!

There are too many factors determining why someone passes on your script other than your talent or the quality of your script. Don't be shy (but don't be defensive) when rejected, call and ask for an honest critique of the script. Thank the story editor for his/her time. If your script is rejected, send it to the next person on the list, and keep sending until you find someone who says yes.

Note: If you receive enough feedback listing the same problems, then you need to rewrite your script before sending it out again. Wait until you have several of the same negative comments, however, because you don't want to tailor your teleplay to someone who's already rejected it.

Let's say your script is received enthusiastically because you've followed the *Animation Scriptwriting: Writer's Road Map* creatively and successfully, showing off your talents as a writer. Then jump in the express lane. You're on your way!

The Pitch

Once you've got the story editor's attention, they will ask you to come in and pitch. You have to pass over this speed bump before entering any of the steps below. So be prepared. When pitching:

1 Show up to the meeting with three to six written springboards (discussed below) to pitch, *not read,* to them.

2 Don't wing your pitch! Rehearse your springboards. Practice pitching, and be animated (pun intended)! You're selling your idea. If you're not excited about it, how can they be?

3 During the pitch, don't throw in character dialogue. You want your jokes to read fresh so save them for the script.

4 Tell the springboard, then follow their lead. If the story editors ask for more detail, tell them more details of the plot and some of the gags as well, but not too many. Again, you want to save these for the script.

5 Be relaxed and listen. Allow them to inject. If they are asking questions, it means they are interested.

You must be flexible in the pitching process, story editors make corrections as you pitch. It isn't a criticism of your pitching style. They best know the needs of their own series, after all, they most likely developed it. Don't get defensive; listen to their suggestions and alter your pitch accordingly.

6 Glean as much information from them as you can. Ask questions, show your interest in the series and in your own ideas.

Story editors are most likely the nicest people you'll ever work with, but please remember, they are under killer deadlines. They can't afford to sit around and wait on you in any step of the process. Be professional.

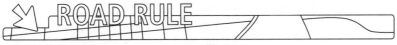

Road Rule #34: BE ON TIME. NO EXCUSES.

As you pitch, the story editor looks to see how well you know story structure, their characters, and the tone of their cartoon series. You want to illustrate you've mastered all three of these points in your pitch which brings us to springboards.

Note: If they do pass on all your ideas, be gracious. You want to pitch to them again. You should have more knowledge after your pitch of what they need for their series. Go develop more springboards, and then set up another pitch meeting with them.

The Springboard

So what exactly is a springboard? It's a three to six sentence idea from which your story "springs." It is your pitch to the story editor, telling what your story is about, and what the character will accomplish or learn in the course of the story. It combines both your moral if you have one (and you will if that is a rule of its cartooniverse) and your central idea, explaining the beginning, middle and end of the story in a few succinct sentences.

In your springboard, capture the flair of the cartoon tunnel. If you develop a springboard for an action tunnel, your springboard should reflect action; if you develop a springboard for a gag tunnel, your springboard should reflect humor.

Road Rule #35: A good springboard always derives from character.

If you are writing a spec episode for *The Simpsons* with Bart as your driver, the story idea will probably "spring" from Bart's next scheme or prank.

In *Johnny Bravo*, the story usually centers around Johnny chasing after a cute "babe."

In *Rugrats*, the story stems from the age of the characters. Thus, the stories mostly "spring" from a first experience to something, like Chuckie's first experience with falling in love (*Cradle Attraction*) or Angelica's introduction to "bad" words (*The Word of the Day*).

In your springboard, you must answer as succinctly and as excitingly as possible, these four road flags before proceeding:

1 Who is the show is about?

2 What does the character want?

3 What or who tries to stop him or her?

4 What will the character achieve in the outcome of the story?

Note: The examples below are *not the original* springboards submitted, but a sample of plausible springboards for the episodes we've discussed in this book.

In the 22 minute format, *Batman, The Day of the Samurai*, the springboard could have been written as follows:

Batman rushes to aid an old master whose star student has been kidnaped by a dark Ninja. The evil Ninja seeks to learn the secret of a special type of martial arts which can kill an opponent by a mere touch. Can Batman save the student and prevent the Ninja from learning the secret destructive combat, or will he fall prey to the Ninja's touch of death?

Note: Since, as an audience, we know Batman will come out the victor in some way, and that he isn't learning anything (not part of his cartooniverse), then end with a powerful or dramatic life v. death scenario which implies strong action.

Does the springboard above pass our four flags? Let's break it down and see.

Flag One: As always, the episode is about Batman.

Flag Two: depicts Batman who wants to return the kidnap victim safely and prevent the Ninja from learning the ancient "Touch of Death" technique.

Flag Three: the Ninja battles to stop Batman.

Flag Four: it's inherent to the show that Batman always comes out on top, even if the villain manages to get away.

In the 11 minute format, *Pepper Ann, The Unusual Suspects*:

It happened one dark and devious afternoon. The Hazelnut Middle School Otter statue is missing. The list of suspects, filled the chalkboard, or at least, half of it. One by one, they crumble as Principal Hickey interrogate Milo, Nicky, Trinket and Dieter, leaving only one possible perpetrator left - Pepper Ann. Will she be unjustly framed for this insidious crime? Or will fate treat her fairly? Probably so, since Principal Hickey discovers he's the guilty one! He sent it out to be cleaned, and forgot, leading the group to realize it's best not to jump to conclusions.

Flag One: the story's about Pepper Ann.

Flag Two: implied that Pepper Ann wants to be found innocent.

Flag Three: Principal Hickey out to get the thief.

Flag Four: That it's best not to jump to conclusions.

In the 7 minute format, *Johnny Bravo's Ape Is Enough*:

Pop and Carl go for their annual trip to the islands. Johnny decides to go native too in order to romance an island girl, but nearly ends up a human sacrifice. Things get worse when he's rescued by a female King Kong who thinks Johnny's the top banana.

Flag One: Johnny (cartooniverse rule).

Flag Two: Johnny wants to find a native sweetheart.

Flag Three: A giant female ape wants Johnny as her sweetie.

Flag Four: not a rule of its cartooniverse.

From *Doug – Doug's Dog's Date*: Something's up with Pork Chop, and Doug's on the tail, or trail, that is. Our ace detective discovers Pork Chop's in love. Dumped by his best friend for a poodle, Doug misses Pork Chop and ponders life with a new pet. When Pork Chop's dumped by his puffy pooch, Doug realizes friends have to stick together.

Exercise #74: Break down the springboard for *Doug*, answering the four springboard questions. Does each follow all four flags?

As you create your springboards, remember that whatever you think of first, that's probably what everyone else thinks up too. Brainstorm for ideas, discarding the first five. Most likely, the sixth or seventh idea will really be something clever and fresh.

For your pitch, you want to develop fifteen springboards, dividing them so you have four to five ideas for each prominent character on the series. Why? Because when you go in to pitch (let's say for *The Simpsons*) you might find the story editor has several Bart stories, but is light (has very few) on Lisa stories. Thus, you can switch, and pitch the five springboards you've created for Lisa Simpson. Don't lose a pitch just because you developed springboards for only one or two of the show's characters (unless the cartooniverse only does story about one character like Batman). In addition, pitch with enthusiasm! You want to convince the story editors to develop your springboards, and get that freelance assignment.

Note: Never pitch all fifteen of your storyboards in one pitch. Get feedback from the story editor, then pitch again at another time.

Road Rule #36: Make sure the springboards you pitch are creative, fresh, and reflect its cartoon tunnel.

If the story editor approves your springboard, you get to continue to the next bump in the road – the premise. Congratulations. This means you're just one step away from getting a *paid* writing assignment.

Exercise #75: Create fifteen springboards for the show you'd like to pitch to; have several springboards per character, and answer all four springboard flags (if applicable). Capture the tone of the genre in each.

The Premise

It's time to turn your springboard into a premise. The premise ranges from a few paragraphs to two pages. It is a synopsis, explaining in a thrilling and fun way, the major plot points (Tow-Away Street, Green Light, U-Turn...) which characters are involved in the story, and the main action and gag sequences in your story. Here is where you demonstrate where the humor and/or action of your episode will derive. In the premise, your characters are capitalized throughout to quickly illustrate who dominates the story.

The premise is your true sell of your story, so put all your effort into making it humorous and exciting. Capture the style of the series. Put in some of the gags or play on words to reflect the humor of your episode.

For your premise, the turn-around time should be one to three days. Story editors don't have time to sit around and wait. Get it back to them as quickly as possible. Remember, they only have so many slots to fill, and other writers will be vying for episodes too so:

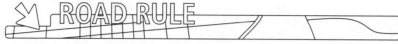

Road Rule #37: MEET YOUR DEADLINES!

Your reputation, in part, is built upon your ability to meet deadlines. The animation industry is a small community. Reputations, both good and bad, spread quickly.

The sample below is an excerpt of the premise I created for RUBY/ SPEARS PRODUCTIONS & ABC. As it was a sequel to an original story I had written (*The Legend of Skull Duggery*) as well as their Halloween episode, I had permission to create two new evil ghosts for the episode.

SKULL DUGGERY RIDES AGAIN

Premise

A stormy night. Lightning flashes and thunder rolls. Suddenly, a lightning bolt strikes Skull Mountain. Rock debris flies out of the Skull's eye sockets. Deep in the bowels of the mountain a shimmer of light breaks through and SKULL DUGGERY'S diabolical laughter fills the mine. SKULL DUGGERY rises amid the rumble, his eyes glowing. An evil smile curls his lips.

GHOST TOWN – sign reads: "Enter At Your Own Death." SKULL DUGGERY rides straight for the Ghouloon. Inside, is the ghastliest, ugliest, meanest group of ghosts west of the Mesa. Duggery reunites with his old friends, DARK FANG and ONE-EYED JACK. DARK FANG is a maniacal wolf with a vampirish quality whereas ONE-EYED JACK is a Jack Rabbit with razor sharp teeth and a madness in one eye (the other one patched). The three vow vengeance against Moo and his Cow Town as they ride off on their skeletal steeds.

BACK AT COW TOWN, everyone prepares for the Halloween Party when bizarre things start to happen, including an invisible stampede that rushes down Main Street – or at least it sounds like one. MOO wants to know what's going on?! In a surprise attack, the GHOST GANG attacks. Before our HEROES can chase them from town, the GHOSTS shoot ghostly winds from their eyes and fingertips, aiming their malevolence at the Tumbleweed Saloon and the General Store. The buildings age, dilapidated with cobwebs and holes. Everyone inside has been aged as well, including MISS LILY! MOO is heart-broken.

MAYOR BULLONEY seizes his chance to get rid of our HEROES once and for all. BULLONEY and his LACKEYS conspire with the GHOSTS, setting a trap for the C.O.W.BOYS, but their trap backfires as the GHOSTS double-cross them and BULLONEY and his SIDEKICKS end up a group of bickering old coots. Now our HEROES must harness the storm's energy in true *BACK TO THE FUTURE* style to get rid of DUGGERY and his GHOSTLY GANG, and break the specter's spell before it's too late!

In this step, you might be asked to rewrite your premise after the story editor's Notes. That's okay, do it. If you can't convince them by the second (or at least the third) draft of your premise, most likely you won't get to proceed to the next speed bump.

The Treatment

Next comes the treatment. If you are asked to do a treatment, then you are being commissioned to write your premise into a script. The story editor will ask you for a deadline. You should take no more than a week to get the treatment to him/her.

Note: The faster you are, the more the story editor will appreciate you. But NEVER sacrifice the quality of your script just to finish it faster. The story editor wants a polished and funny treatment rather than something that looks rushed and not well thought out.

In this step, you break down the action of each sequential scene, explaining what it is and what it accomplishes. It is in essence, your treatment which contains all the locations and characters that will be in your script. Again, always leave the scene with the character knowing more and/or achieving more than when s/he entered it.

Be brief in your treatment. Tell the story as succinctly as possible. Begin each scene with its slugline. Enter the scene late and leave early here as well. Block out all the action and gag sequences in your story. You can sprinkle it with a few (not many) lines of dialogue if you want.

Just as in your premise, in your treatment, always capitalize your characters. Your treatment can range in length from about 18 to 24 pages for a 22 minute script, 10 to 14 in a 11 minute script, 4 to 8 pages in a 7 minute script.

Before proceeding forward to script, you might receive Notes and be asked to do a second treatment, OR asked to move onto the script and incorporate the changes there, OR the story editor might rewrite your treatment due to limited time. Don't take this personally either. Once s/he's done this, they will send you on to script.

Below is an excerpt from Act One from my treatment of "*Skull Duggery Rides Again*," which sets up the revenge story. The first seven scenes included:

C.O.W. BOYS OF MOO MESA

Skull Duggery Rides Again!

ACT ONE

EXT. SKULL MOUNTAIN – NIGHT

A stormy night. Lightning flashes and thunder rolls. A lightning bolt strikes Skull Mountain. Rock debris shoots out of the Skull's eye sockets. Deep in the bowels of the mountain, a shimmer of moonlight breaks through and SKULL DUGGERY'S diabolical laughter fills the mine. Amid the rubble, SKULL DUGGERY rises, his eyes glowing. An evil smile curls his lips.

INT. BIG RED BARN – SAME

On a farm outside of Cow Town, a pumpkin patch lays next to a large red barn. Inside, MOO and MISS LILY hang orange and black decorations. Through the barn doors, lightning flashes.

COWLORADO puts on his black mask and cape, all decked out like a Musketeer while DAKOTA hauls in several sacks of apples for bobbing. COWLORADO proudly displays his costume, leaping up onto a couple of hay bales. They can be the Three Musketeers, COWLORADO, of course, the dashing D'Artagnan. He swings across the barn in true Musketeer style, using a rope that's been strung to the center beam to hang lanterns.

His sword slashes the already hanging decorations which all fall onto DAKOTA. COWLORADO attempts a smile, "Ooops." DAKOTA snorts, crepe paper hanging from his horns. Moo smiles, reminding DAKOTA, "Why even you were a calf once."

Through the doors, a large pumpkin with feet waddles inside Charlie Chaplin style. Off comes the large pumpkin, CODY smiling. MOO grins, "That pumpkin's a bit big for a calf-pint." CODY looks up at DAKOTA who tries to untangle himself from the decorations. "Whoa, what a cool costume!" CODY exclaims. COWLORADO smells garlic? CODY pulls out a string of garlic – "Jest in case any real ghosts and goblins appear on Halloween," he'll be prepared to fend them off. Thunder booms and lightning fills the sky, grabbing their attention. MOO notes, if the storm keeps up, it's likely to be a Halloween they won't forget.

EXT. GHOST TOWN – STILL NIGHT

SKULL DUGGERY saunters into the edge of the cobwebbed, tumbleweeded, dilapidated town. Cracked and weathered tombstones tower in the moonlight. A "No Vacancy" sign hangs on the cemetery gate. As SKULL DUGGERY makes it into town, another sign reads: "Enter At Your Own Death." SKULL DUGGERY snickers as he heads straight for the Ghouloon.

INT. GHOULOON – SAME

Inside the ghostly saloon, is the ghastliest, ugliest, orneriest group of GHOSTS west of the Mesa. In the corner, a RACCOON with ghoulish dark circles around his eyes plays an organ instead of a piano, his melody straight out of a Bela Lugosi movie.

DARK FANG and ONE-EYED JACK RABID play poker. DARK FANG is a maniacal wolf, a vampirish quality about him with his long fangs and cape (which conjures up ghostly weather when opened.) ONE-EYED JACK is a Jack Rabbit with razor sharp teeth, mangy ears and a madness in his eye (the other one patched). From his good eye, a laser beam can shoot, crumbling his targets into little heaps of dust and debris.

At their table, a PORCUPINE accuses DARK FANG of cheating. Silence fills the Ghouloon as DARK FANG rises and the two face off in a showdown. The PORCUPINE draws, but DARK FANG flings open his cape. A cold wintery wind blasts the PORCUPINE, rolling him into a little ball. He spins out the Ghouloon doors, a frost-bitten tumbleweed. DARK FANG howls in delight.

EXT. GHOULOON – SAME

The winterized, prickly ghost tumbles past SKULL DUGGERY. DUGGERY grins sinisterly as he steps onto the sidewalk.

INT. GHOULOON – SAME

The other GHOSTLY PATRONS, now frostbitten and teeth chattering, quickly turn back to their own card games. SKULL DUGGERY flings the doors open dramatically and enters. He spots his old pals who scoop up the poker money. ONE-EYED JACK orders a round of ghostly brew, smoke spiraling from the mugs as the threesome reunite. SKULL DUGGERY says he's got a town to haunt and a bull to bury – are they in or not?

Before they can reply, a timid *NON-GHOST* GROUNDHOG steps hesitantly into the Ghouloon, holding his hat nervously. All the GHOSTS turn and stare at this out of place "guest." The RACCOON stops playing. The GROUNDHOG stutters. He's lost – "Anyone know the way to San Jose?"

ONE-EYED JACK says they don't like strangers, beaming his one good eye and vaporizing the floor under the GROUNDHOG. The little guy drops through the floor and out of sight. ONE-EYED JACK RAPID says "Let's go kick some bull!" SKULL DUGGERY vows his vengeance – "By the time I'm finished with MARSHALL MOO and his little Cow Town, there won't be nothin' left for the vultures."

And so it would continue. You get the idea. As you can see, you are really fleshing out your story here. By the time you finish your treatment, you'll have most of your script written. You'll have many of your gags and should have broken down all your action. Once you get the go-ahead to write your script, you'll mainly just be adding the dialogue and more gags.

Note: Don't include images or drawings in any of the phases.

The Beat Outline

The beat outline further divides your story into sections so the story editor can scrutinize each plot point, action sequence and gag. You won't always have to do this next step. Depending on your story, you might have to go through this phase in order to illustrate the breakdown of action and gags so the story editor can estimate the approximate screen time of animating these sequences. If he does ask for a beat outline, then you will take your treatment, and format it like the beat outline below, breaking up each scene into specific parts.

The beat outline generally runs about 15 pages in length for a 22 minute script, and about 8 pages for an 11 minute script, 4 pages for a 7 minute script. Once you've handed in this, the story editor will give you Notes, and you'll be sent to script.

If I had converted my treatment of *Skull Duggery Rides Again* into a beat outline, it would look like this:

C.O.W. BOYS OF MOO MESA

Skull Duggery Rides Again!

ACT ONE

I. EXT. SKULL MOUNTAIN – NIGHT

    A. A stormy night.

        1. Lightning flashes and thunder rolls.

        2. A lightning bolt strikes Skull Mountain.

        3. Rock debris shoots out of the Skull's eye sockets.

    B. Deep in the bowels of the mountain, a shimmer of moonlight breaks through and SKULL DUGGERY'S diabolical laughter fills the mine.

    C. Amid the rubble, SKULL DUGGERY rises, his eyes glowing. An evil smile curls his lips.

II. INT. BIG RED BARN – SAME

A. On a farm outside of Cow Town, a pumpkin patch lays next to a large red barn. Inside, MOO and MISS LILY hang orange and black decorations. Through the barn doors, lightning flashes.

1. COWLORADO puts on his black mask and cape, all decked out like a Musketeer.

2. DAKOTA hauls in several sacks of apples for bobbing.

3. COWLORADO proudly displays his costume, leaping up onto a couple of hay bales. They can be the Three Musketeers, COWLORADO, of course, the dashing D'Artagnan.

4. He swings across the barn in true Musketeer style, using a rope that's been strung to the center beam to hang lanterns.

5. His sword slashes the already hanging decorations which all fall onto DAKOTA.

6. COWLORADO attempts a smile, "Ooops."

7. DAKOTA snorts, crepe paper hanging from his horns.

8. Moo smiles, reminding DAKOTA, "Why even you were a calf once."

B. Through the doors, a large pumpkin with feet waddles inside Charlie Chaplin style.

1. Off comes the large pumpkin, CODY smiling.

2. MOO grins, "That pumpkin's a bit big for a calf-pint."

3. CODY looks up at DAKOTA who tries to untangle himself from the decorations – "Whoa, what a cool costume!" CODY exclaims.

4. COWLORADO smells garlic?

5. CODY pulls out a string of garlic – "Jest in case any real ghosts and goblins appear on Halloween," he'll be prepared to fend them off.

C. Thunder booms and lightning fills the sky, grabbing their attention.

    1. MOO notes, if the storm keeps up, it's likely to be a Halloween they won't forget.

I would continue converting my treatment into the beat outline until I had outlined all three acts this way. You're just breaking up gags and action sequences so the story editor can determine if all the action you're writing in the script can be animated within your 22, 11, or 7 minutes.

Now, finally you get to write the script. This is the best step of all because it is the step you get paid for – Yabba Dabba Do!

The Script

Applause! You have arrived as an animation writer. You're going to get paid for all your hard endeavors. In this step, you take your treatment and add the dialogue to it. Follow all the Road Rules listed in this book, use your comedy cones and dialogue devices to create the best animated script you can write.

Generally, this step has three stages to it. You will be asked to write the first draft, then asked to do a rewrite, followed by a polish. Your pay scale will be broken down similarly as well. That is, you'll be paid for the script, then the rewrite and then the polish, most likely. Sometimes your deal might ask for an additional rewrite or polish. Don't do more rewrites or polishes than you are asked to do in your contract. Since story editors are writers themselves, they've been where you are, and they're not likely to ask you for anything that isn't fair, but just beware.

Throughout each speed bump in this process, strive to improve your work, incorporating all the Notes you get from the story editors and making them fit naturally into your script. Dedication means a lot to story editors. The more work you do, the less they have to do, and the more they'll appreciate your efforts.

When you turn in your teleplay, you want to include a cast list, location list and a title page for production purposes. Your cast list contains the title of the episode (center) and all the cast (flush left). If you are introducing new characters, then you also include their character tags with their names. Your location list consists of the slugline (minus DAY/ NIGHT) of each location used in your script (flush left). If you introduce a new location, then you want to include a one or two line description as well after listing it. Your title page should list the series, the episode, the writer (all centered) and the logline which is basically your springboard or a summation of your springboard. It consists of one to three sentences.

In Conclusion

Get your scripts out there, get them read. Establish a network of contacts, because more than talent and more than luck, it's WHO YOU KNOW! Build and keep relationships with story editors. They bounce from series to series, so keep tabs on them. To network with animation producers, hang out at comic book conventions. They will be there looking for those marquee concepts to develop into a profitable series. There's a large comic book convention in San Diego, California every August, and there are several throughout the year in Texas. Check the state you live in to find comic book conventions near you. Read various Animation magazines for up to date information. Get to know the animation industry. Your career depends upon it.

Each studio has its own signature style. Find the one that matches your talents as an animation writer. Your career is what YOU make it. There'll be bumps along the way, but if you have the endurance to stick with it, and follow your *Animation Scriptwriting: Writer's Road Map* animation writing can be a very rewarding and fun career. So get to it. The open road awaits you.

Glossary

antagonist: the villain or character who opposes the driver (hero).

alliteration: a repetition of initial sounds in adjacent words or syllables.

A-story: main plot of your story.

B-story: subplot of your story, generally the character story.

backstory: all the information about your character and his/her relationships to other characters that takes place before your story begins.

beat outline: the fourth phase of the animation process; it is not always a required step. The beat outline will include a more specific breakdown of your story's action and gag sequences.

b.g.: is used in scripts to abbreviate "background."

breaking the fourth wall: when a character turns and speaks directly into the camera to the audience.

broadcaster-relatable: when a story does not break any of the specific broadcaster's guidelines in regards to safety and legality.

build-up: the sequential construction of your story which builds tension and suspense through its action and/or comedy.

cartoon bible: a document of 30 – 45 pages of written information on the cartoon series. It includes character descriptions and relationships, sample springboards, any myths or legends which set up the cartoon, a summary of the series, descriptions of the sets and locations, and all the rules cartooniverse. Also known as a **series bible**.

cartooniverse: the world in which the cartoon characters live.

cartoon lineage: a "family" link from a classic cartoon character to a new one.

cartoon physical feats: feats performed by cartoon characters which defy the laws of the universe and which humans cannot perform without grave consequences.

cartoon tunnel: the genre of a cartoon.

central idea: the idea which sums up in one or two sentences who and what your story is about.

central question avenue: the question which spins the story and which is answered in the climax.

character arc: the learning curve (arc) of a character, i.e., what a character learns in the course of the story, although in animation, it will not change the character generally.

character compass: the major and minor character traits which establish a character's personality. It includes positive as well as negative traits.

character dipstick: a list of important moments in a character's life, and how they shaped his/her personality. It also includes any important relationship which shapes/has shaped the character, his/her backstory, and his/her physical traits.

character tag: the unique and fun description of a character. Used only when introducing a new character.

character tic: a trait or distinction given only to that particular character.

city block: a story sequence composed of ten – twenty streets (scenes). It has its own beginning, middle, and end with obstacles or dilemmas which confront the driver.

cliche: phrases which we have heard so often they become trite.

climax: the dramatic clash or confrontation for the driver which occurs at the end of the story.

cold calls: networking, that is, making phone calls to story editors in order to introduce yourself and request permission to submit a script to their show in hopes of gaining a freelance assignment.

comeback: a sarcastic or humorous response by one character to another.

comedy cones: mechanisms of humor, gag techniques for your script.

dead air: when there is not enough dialogue or action in the script, and as a result, the animation director must hold on a reaction of a character to fill time.

dialogue block: the lines of dialogue that make up a character's speech block.

dialogue devices: writer's tools to jazz up dialogue, making it more interesting.

dissolve: to fade two adjacent scenes together, overlapping one image over the other. This is used mostly to denote a passage of time.

euphemism: the substitution of a cultural phrase in order to shortly express a certain idea. It is a phrase which is taken interpretively, not literally. For example, "crying over spilt milk" is a euphemism which implies one should not cry over something that has already happened and cannot be changed. It doesn't mean a person is literally crying over spilt milk.

exposition: information needed by the audience to understand the story or a character's motivations.

Est. shot: establishing shot; this is sometimes used to set up a location.

EXT.: exterior; describes the location in the slugline and is always abbreviated in capital letters.

falling rocks: the obstacles hurled at your driver during your story.

flashback: a scene which flashes back in time; a technique used to give exposition.

freelance: to write by contract basis, assignment by assignment, rather than writing on staff.

gag: a quip, prank, laugh-provoking remark, or visually humorous joke.

gag humor: humor derived from gags.

genre: the category of the story being told, i.e., a comedy, a western, a mystery...

graphing: to outline scene by scene a cartoon or script, listing the essence of each scene, who is in the scene, where and when the scene takes place, and what time the scene falls in the episode (by minutes) or script (by page).

green light: the scene in Act One where the driver (hero) must commit to the story. S/he speeds into the action full speed ahead.

hang time: when a cartoon character races off a cliff and "hangs" in midair before falling.

hero/heroine: the driver of your story, your story's protagonist. This is the character the audience roots for throughout your story.

high-concept: a story idea which can be conveyed in one or two sentences with a hook that makes the story easily recognized as becoming a profitable cartoon series.

hook: a twist that makes the story idea fresh and original.

INT.: interior; describes the location in the slugline; always abbreviated in capital letters.

juxtapose: to place side by side in comparison.

kid-relatable: when a script is written so as to be relatable to children.

logline: a one to three sentence summation of your springboard. It basically states who and what the story is about in a flashy way.

live-action: a story which doesn't involve animation.

locale: the exterior place in which the scene occurs.

music montage: a series of scenes without dialogue where music plays over the images. Often used to illustrate time passing, characters falling in love, etc.

no outlet: the scene (street) in which the driver must make a choice which implies severe consequences. It is a street that once he/she drives onto, there is no going back; the road of no return.

oblique scene: to write a scene that is unexpected, surprising the audience and/or a character.

one-two payoff: this gag incorporates an action-reaction, and then an unexpected action. The set-up of the gag is the one-two, then the payoff comes, topping the gag.

on ramp: the last street or scene in Act One of a 22 minute formatted script. It includes the story signposts, and is the first act out.

parallel plotting: when the subplot parallels the main plot, telling the same story, just through another character's point of view.

parody: a comical or satirical imitation of someone or something.

pay-off: when a writer "pays off" or completes the set-up of the gag by topping it with a gag that is humorous and unexpected.

pitch: to tell a story idea to story editors as succinctly and enthusiastically as possible, capturing the tone of their cartoon series.

pit stop principle: taking several days to several weeks off to refuel your imagination and therefore, come back to your script with fresh energy.

plot: is the structure of your story, the storyline. There are three basic plots: man vs nature, man vs man, man vs himself.

point-of-view: (POV) from whose perspective the story is told.

premise: the second phase in animation writing, it is a brief summary of a story, including all major plot points and action sequences. It should also include all the characters in the story, and capture the tone of the cartoon in the most exciting way. This is the written sales pitch of your story idea. It runs a few paragraphs to two pages.

props: objects within the scene or that may appear in the scene to be used by your characters.

prose: the description or action in the scene, i.e. everything on the script page that isn't a slugline or dialogue or a character name.

prose blocks: the description of a scene or action; the lines that are blocked together which make up your prose.

protagonist: the main character of the story, the driver.

pun: the humorous use of a word in a way that suggests two or more interpretations.

put-down: name-calling and/or a type of insult.

query letter: a letter sent to acquire permission to submit a sample script. It should include point of the letter, information about the writer, a brief synopsis of the script, and any acclaim the script has garnered.

rest area: a scene in which the character and/or audience can take a moment to rest from the tension of the plot. It serves as an emotional moment or comical moment for a character.

resolution: the conclusion or result of the storyline.

road map: the writer's outline.

round robin of villains: when a series has several rotating villains.

running gags: a gag which repeats through a scene, episode or series.

sample script: a script you write, not to sell, but to show off your talents as a writer and get you a freelance assignment.

scene: (street) a story unit. A scene changes any time the story moves to a new location or a new time.

screen directions: written in capital letters; these are shots listed in the script to visually guide the animator. For example, CU (a close up) or LS (a long shot).

screen narration: information given to the audience via a character speaking directly to the audience, or written visually on the screen.

segue: switching to a new scene.

series bible: a document of 30 – 45 pages of written information on the cartoon series. It includes character descriptions and relationships, sample springboards, any myths or legends which set up the cartoon, a summary of the series, descriptions of the sets and locations, and all the rules cartooniverse. Also known as a **cartoon bible**.

sets: the physical background of an interior scene. For example, the kitchen in *Dexter's Laboratory* would include the table, chairs, and kitchen cabinets. It does not include the characters or props in the scene.

sidekick: a character who interacts only with the hero or villain.

signature lines: a line of dialogue that identifies with only one certain character.

slugline: the line which introduces each scene. It is always written in capital letters and includes whether the scene is exterior or interior, its location, and the time of day. For example: INT. SEWER PIPES – MIDNIGHT or EXT. CENTRAL PARK - LATE AFTERNOON.

sound effects (SFX): the sounds heard in a cartoon.

spec script: a script written in hopes of selling on speculation.

spoof: to poke fun of something or someone in a good-natured manner.

springboard: a three to six sentence idea which includes what your story is about, what the character will accomplish in the story, combining the moral and central idea. It has a beginning, middle and end, and should capture the tone of the cartoon series.

story editor: the person who develops and oversees the cartoon series.

story signposts: turning points in the plot, several of which, must occur at the end of Act One and/or Act Two in your various plot structures to increase dramatic tension in your story structure.

street: in this book, a street equals one scene or a series of very short scenes.

tag: the description given to a character when he/she is first introduced in the script. The tag itself is not capitalized, but the character's name is (but only the *first* time he/she appears on the page.

talking heads: when cartoon characters sit or stand chatting, and there is no movement except for their facial expressions.

target age: the age you are trying to reach in your script.

teleplay: a script written exclusively for television.

teaser: a scene or series of short scenes which introduce the cartoon episode in an exciting way to grab the audience's attention.

ticking clock: a story device which sets up tension and a need for immediate action by the character. It dictates that a character perform a certain action by a specific time, or a grave consequence will occur. Often this device is set into motion by the story's villain or antagonist.

topper: a gag or line of dialogue which "tops" (more witty or humorous than) the previous gag.

tow-away street: the story's catalyst; the scene in Act One in which the driver is towed or pulled into the story.

treatment: the third phase in the animation writing process. Here, you break down the action and humor of each scene sequentially, explaining in paragraph form what the scene is about and what is accomplished. It will contain all the characters and scenes that will be in your script. It can also include a few lines of dialogue if desired.

true north: the character's type, that is, is the character a race car driver, taxi cab driver, demolition driver, or anti-car driver?

try-fails: gag sequences in which a character tries to achieve a goal, fails, then tries again and fails again.

turnaround time: the length of time from when you are sent off to write (a premise, outline, treatment, script) to when you turn it in to the story editor.

u-turn: the scene which turns the story in a totally new or unexpected direction.

verbal parody: a comical or satirical *verbal* imitation of someone or something.

voice over: (VO) is used when a character's voice is heard, but the character is not seen on the screen or not seen on the screen speaking the words being heard.

winding road: the subplot which winds through the story, reflecting the story's main plot line.

Cartoonography

Below you'll find only the distribution company listed on a few of the cartoons. This is because only the series name was mentioned, and not a particular episode.

Ace Ventura Pet Detective – executive producer James G. Robinson, Robert P. Mandell, producer Eleanor Kearney, story editors Tom Mason and Dan Danko, Seth MacFarlane, storyboard supervisor Cullen Blaine. *Ace In Space* written by Bill Matheny. Warner Brotherss.

Addams Family – Warner Brothers.

Anatole – based on a book by Eve Titus & inspired by the illustrations of Paul Galdone, executive producers Michael Hirsch, Patrick Loubert, Clive Smith, Pascal Herold, Ellen Freyer, Linda Jassin, story editor Susan Snooks, storyboard supervisor Ted Bastien. *Mystery of the Dancing Ghost* written by Mary Crawford and Alan Templeton. Nelvana Ltd. CBS Productions.

Batman – based on D.C. comic characters, *Batman* created by Bob Kane, executive producers Jean MacCurdy, Tom Ruegger, producers Alan Burnett, Eric Radomski, Bruce W. Timm, story editor Michael Reeves. *Day of the Samuri* written by Steve Perry, storyboard by Michael Diederich, Mike Goguen, Gary Graham, Brad Rader, Bruce W. Timm, Mark Wallace. Warner Brothers.

Beetlejuice – executive producers David Geffen, Tim Burton, producers Michael Hirsh, Patrick Loubert, Clive A. Smith, story editors Patsy Cameron, Tedd Anasti. *Bad Neighbor Beetlejuice* written by Therese Naugle, storyboard by John Flagg, Bill Perkins, Raymond Jaffelice, Eric Chu, Alan Bunce, Keith Ingham, Neil Hunter. Geffen & Nelvana. Warner Brothers.

Blasters – based on educational software, executive producers Patrick Laubert, Michael Hirsch, Clive A. Smith, James Wang, Cathy Siegel, story editor Hugh Duffy, storyboard coordinator Allan Parkera. *Sound Advice* written by Ben Joseph. *Supreme Commander of the Universe* written by Dave Dias. Nelvana Ltd & CBS Productions.

Count Duckula – Cartoon from Japan.

Courage The Cowardly Dog – executive producer John R. Dilworth, producer Robert Winthrop, head writer David Steven Cohen, storyboard supervisor Bob Miller. *Shirley the Medium* written by Luc Latulippe. *The Hunchback of Nowhere* written by Irvin S. Bauer, storyboard by Dave Simons. *The Gods Must Be Goosey* written by David Steven Cohen, storyboard by Michael Wetterhahn, John Flagg, J.P. Dillard, Pilar Newton. Stretch Films Inc.

Cow & Chicken – created by David Feiss. *The Penalty Wheel* story by David Feiss, Michael Ryan, storyboard by Nora Johnson. *The Baby Sitter* story by Steve Marmel, storyboard by Nora Johnson. *Night of the Ed* story by David Feiss, Michael Ryan, storyboard by Maxwell Atoms. Hanna-Barbera Productions.

C.O.W. Boys Of Moo Mesa – executive producers Lee Gunther, Michael Wahl, producer Mitch Schauer, storyboard supervisor Karl Toerge. *The Legend of Skull Duggery* written by Marilyn Webber. *Night of the Cowgoyle* written by Marilyn Webber. *Skull Duggery Rides Again* written by Marilyn Webber. Gunther-Wahl Productions & King World.

Dark Water – Hanna-Barbera Productions.

Darkwing Duck – Walt Disney TV Animation.

Dexter's Laboratory – produced and created Genndy Tartakovsky, *Don't Be A Baby* story and storyboard by Mike Stern. *Dee Dee's Tail* written by Kevin Kaliher. *G.I.R.L. Squad*: written by Rumen Patck, storyboard by Andy Bialk. *Topped Off* story and storyboard by Chris Savino. Hanna-Barbera Productions.

Doug – created by Jim Jinkins, original characters by Jim Jinkins and Joe Aaron, producer Melanie Gvisanti, story editors Bradley Kesden, Skip Shephard. *Doug's Dog's Date* written by Betty G. Birney, storyboard by Tony Eastman. Jumbo Pictures Inc.

Dragon Ball Z – based on original comics by Akira Toriyama, executive producer Gen Fukunaga, Cindy Brennan Fukunaga, producers Daniel Cocanougher, Barry Watson, story editor Christopher Neel, *Trouble on Aria* written by Christopher Neel and Chris Forbis. FUNimation Productions Inc.

Dr. Katz – created by Tom Snyder, Jonathan Katz. Executive producers Tom Snyder, Tim Braine, Nancy Geller. Producers Jonathan Katz. Written by Jonathan Katz and staff writers. HBO, Downtown Prods.

Flintstones – Producers Joseph Barbera and William Hanna. *Hawaiian Spy*: written by Jack Raymond. Storyboard by Ed Love, Carlo Vinci, Hugh Fraser, Ed Parks. Hanna-Barbera Productions.

Garfield & Friends – created by Jim Davis, executive producer Phil Roman, Lee Mendelson, Jim Davis, producer Bob Nesler, storyboard by Gary Conrad, Alan Zegler, Mitch Schauer. *Annoying Things* written by Mark Evanier. Film Roman Productions.

Goof Troop – Walt Disney TV Animation.

Gundam Wing – Sunrise TV Asahi.

Hey Arnold – created by Craig Bartlett, developed by Craig Bartlett, Joe Ansolabehere, Steve Viksten, executive producer Craig Bartlett, co-producer Rachel Lipman, Steve Viksten, Joseph Purdy, story editor Antoinette Stella. *Career Day* written by Jonathan Greenberg, storyboard by Derek Drymon, Rob Porter. Viacom.

Inspector Gadget – DIC Entertainment.

The Jetsons – executive producers Joseph Hanna and William Barbera, producers Berny Wolf and Jeff Hall, story editors Don Nelson and Arthur Alsberg. *Father/Daughter Dance* written by Haskell Barkin. Hanna Barbera Productions.

Johnny Bravo – created by Van Partible, producers Gary Hartle, Jed Spingarn. *Ape Is Enough* written by Jed Spingarn, Gene Grille, Wendell Morris, storyboard by Michael Diederich. *A Boy and His Bird* written by Jed Spingarn, Gene Grille, storyboard by Neal Sternecky. *Johnny and the Beanstalk* written by Russell Calabrese, Dave Schwartz, storyboard by Dave Schwartz. *Under the Big Flop*, written by Michael Ryan. Hanna Barbera Productions.

Jonny Quest – Hanna-Barbera Productions.

King Of The Hill – 20th Century FOX.

The Little Mermaid – producer Jamie Mitchell, co producers/story editors Tedd Anasti, Patsy Cameron, storyboard by Holly Forsyth, John Dorman, George Goode. *The Great Sebastian* written by Tedd Anasti, Patsy Cameron. Walt Disney TV Animation.

Looney Tunes – Hare Conditioned: story by Tedd Pierce, storyboard by Ken Harris, Ben Washam, Basil Davidovich, Lloyd Vaughan. *Southern Fried Rabbit*: story by Warren Foster, storyboard by Arthur Davis, Manuel Perez, Ken Champin, Virgil Ross. Warner Brothers.

Madeline – based on characters by Ludwig Bemelmans, executive producers Andy Heyward, Robby London, Saul Cooper, Pancho Kohner, producer Stan Phillips, story editor Judy Rothman Rofe. DIC Animation.

Merrie Melodies – Daffy Duck in *A Birth of a Notion*: Warner Brothers.

Muppet Babies – Jim Henson Production.

The New Adventures Of Winnie The Pooh – producer Karl Geurs, story editor Mark Zaslove, storyboard designers Holly Forsyth, Kurt Anderson, storyboard designers Hank Tucker, Bob Kline. *How Much is that Rabbit in the Window?* story by Mark Zaslove, teleplay by Dev Ross. *Cleanliness is Next to Impossible* teleplay by Dev Ross, Bruce Talkington, Mark Zaslove. *Tigger Is the Mother of Invention* Walt Disney TV Animation.

PB & J Otter – executive producer Jim Jinkins, David Campbell, producers JoEllyn Marlow, story editor Jeff Kindley, Storyboard supervisor Siobhan Mullen. Walt Disney TV Animation.

Peanuts – created by Charles Schultz.

Pepper Ann – created by Sue Rose, based on a character created by Paul Rugg, executive producer Sue Rose, Peter Hastings, producer John A. Smith, co-producer Nahnatchka Khan, storyboard Alfred Gonzales, Lyndon Ruddy, Wendy Wester. *The Unusual Suspects*: written by Mirith J. Colao. *Have You Ever Been Unsupervised?* written by Matthew Negrete & Nahnatchka Khan. *Snot's Your Mother's Music* written by Roger Reitzel. Walt Disney TV Animation.

Pink Panther – United Artists Corporation.

Pok'emon – Viz Communications. Warner Bros.

Powerpuff Girls – created by Craig McCracken, *Stuck Up, Up & Away*: written by Jason Butler Rote, Amy Keating Rogers, storyboard by Paul Rudish. Hanna- Barbera Productions.

A Pup Named Scooby Doo – Hanna-Barbera Productions.

Reboot – executive creative consultant Ian Pearson, story editor Lane Raichert, storyboard supervision Blair Peters. *Infected* story by Gavin Blair, Ian Pearson, Phil Mitchell, Lane Raichert, written by Martin Borycki, storyboard by William Lau. *Identity Crisis*: story by Ganin Blair, Paul Mitchell, Ian Pearson, written by Jono Howard. Mainframe Entertainment Alliance.

Rescue Heroes – executive producers Michael Hirsch, Patrick Loubert, Cliver Smith, James Wang, story editor Rhonda Smiley. *Cave-In* written by Rhonda Smiley. Nelvana Ltd.

Rugrats – created by Arlene Klasky, Gabor Gsupo, Paul Germain, executive producers Gabor Gsupo, Arlene Klasky, producer Geraldine Clark, senior story editor Peter Gaffney, Jonathan Greenberg, story editor Rachel Lipman, storyboard by Raymond Johnson, Ron Campell, John Holmquist, Dexter Reed, Kelly James, Jeff Scott, Toni Vain, Debbie Baber. *Moving Away* written by Peter Gaffney, Paul Germain, Jonathan Greenberg, Rachel Lipman, Drew Brothestein. *Cradle Attraction* written by Peter Gaffney, Paul Germain, Jonathan Greenberg, Rachel Lipman. *The Word of the Day*: written by Vinny Montello, Steve Ochs. Klasky Gsupo Inc.

Sabrina – based on characters appearing in Archie Comics, executive producer Savage Steve Holland, Paula Hart, Andy Heyward, Robby London, Michael Maliani, producers Michael Silberkleit and Richard Goldwater. *Truth or Scare* written by Steve Holland, Kevin Murphy. DIC Entertainment.

Scooby Doo – Hanna Barbera Productions.

The Simpsons – created by Matt Groenig, developed by James L. Brooks, Matt Groenig, Sam Simon, executive producers James L. Brooks, Sam Simon, Matt Groenig, Al Jean & Mike Reiss, producer Jon Vitti, John Swartzwelder, Jeff Martin, Conan O'Brien, Frank Mula, David M. Stern,

Richard Raynis. *I Love Lisa* written by Frank Mula. *Homer Simpson in 'Kidney Trouble'* written by John Swartzwelder. (*Homer Alone, Stark Raving Dad, Much Abu About Nothing*) 20th Century Fox.

South Park – created by Trey Parker, Matt Stone, *City on the...* written by Trey Park, Nancy M. Pimental, staff writer David Goodman; *Summer Sucks*: written by Nancy M. Pimental, Trey Parker.

Space Ghost – executive producer Keith Croffort, Mike Lazzo, produced by Michael Cahill. Written by Matt Maiellaro, Jim Fortier, Dave Willis. *The Brilliant Three* Bill Faulkner. William Street.

Tale Spin – Walt Disney TV Animation.

The Thornberry's – created by Arlene Klasky, Gabor Gsupo, Steve Pepoon, David Silverman, Stephen Sustarsic, storyboard by Robert Goodin, Michael D. Kenny, Ron Noble, producer Christine Ferriter, story editors Kate Boutilier, David Regal, storyboard by Albert Calleros, John Fountain, Shawn Murray, Bob Taylor, Steve Loter. *The Temple of Eliza* written by Barbara Herndon and Jill Gorey. *Forget Me Not*: written by Elean Horwitz and Kate Boutilier. Klasky Gsupo Inc.

Tiny Toon Adventures – executive producer Steven Speilberg, producer Tom Ruegger, story editor Paul Dini, storyboard by Chris Otsuki, Alfred Gimeno, Jim Willoughby, Lew Saw. *Rent-A-Friend* written by Jim Reardon. *Bunny Daze* written by Barry Caldwell. Warner Brothers.

Wacky Racers – Hanna-Barbera Producers.

What-A-Mess – DIC Entertainment.

Winnetoons – German Pilot. Animationstudio Ludewig.

Yo Yogi! – Hanna-Barbera Productions.

Filmography

101 Hundred And One Dalmatians – based on the book *A Hundred And One Dalmatians* by Dodie Smith, story by Bill Peet. Walt Disney Productions.

The Little Mermaid – produced by Howard Ashman and John Musker, written and directed by John Musker and Ron Clements. Walt Disney Productions.

Toy Story – executive producers Edwin Catmull, Steve Jobs, produced by Ralph Guggenheim, Bonnie Arnold, original story by John Lasseter, Pete Docter, Andrew Stanton, Joe Ranft, screenplay by Joss Whedon, Andrew Stanton, Joel Cohen and Alec Sokolow, directed by John Lasseter. A Pixar Production. Walt Disney Productions.

Jaws – novel by Peter Benchley, s: Peter Benchley and Carl Gottlieb, d: Steven Speilberg, p: Richard D. Zanuck and David Brown. Universal Studios.

Raiders of The Lost Ark – story by George Lucas, s: Willard Huyck & Gloria Katz, d: Steven Speilberg, p: Robert Watts. Paramount Pictures.

Note: There are many more names too numerous to list for each of the above cartoon episodes. Never the less, their contributions are just as noteworthy and important as those names listed above.

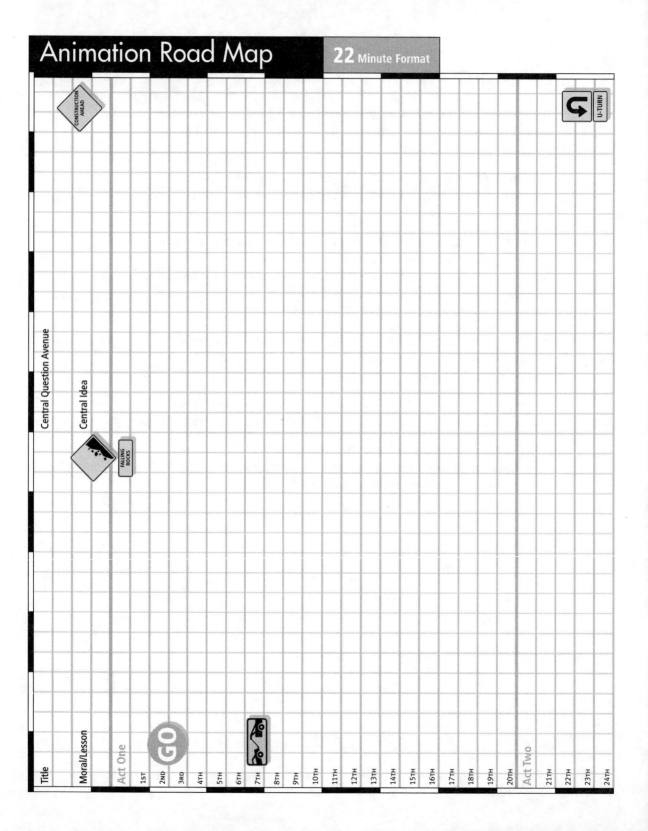

Animation Road Map

22 Minute Format

CONSTRUCTION AHEAD

U-TURN

Central Question Avenue

Central Idea

FALLING ROCKS

Title

Moral/Lesson

Act One

GO

1ST
2ND
3RD
4TH
5TH
6TH
7TH
8TH
9TH
10TH
11TH
12TH
13TH
14TH
15TH
16TH
17TH
18TH
19TH
20TH

Act Two

21ST
22ND
23RD
24TH

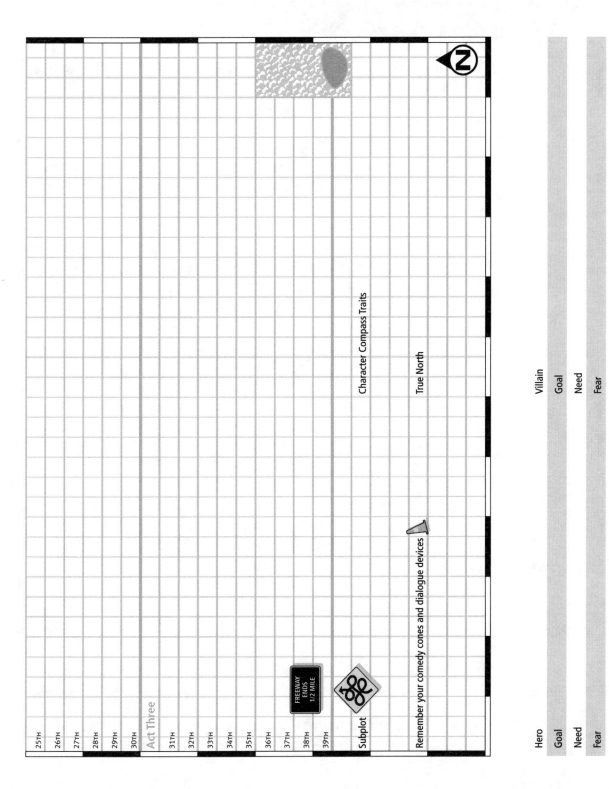

25TH
26TH
27TH
28TH
29TH
30TH

Act Three

31ST
32ND
33RD
34TH
35TH
36TH
37TH
38TH
39TH

FREEWAY
ENDS
1/2 MILE

Subplot

Character Compass Traits

True North

Remember your comedy cones and dialogue devices

N

Hero

Villain

Goal

Goal

Need

Need

Fear

Fear

Animation Road Map — **11** Minute Format

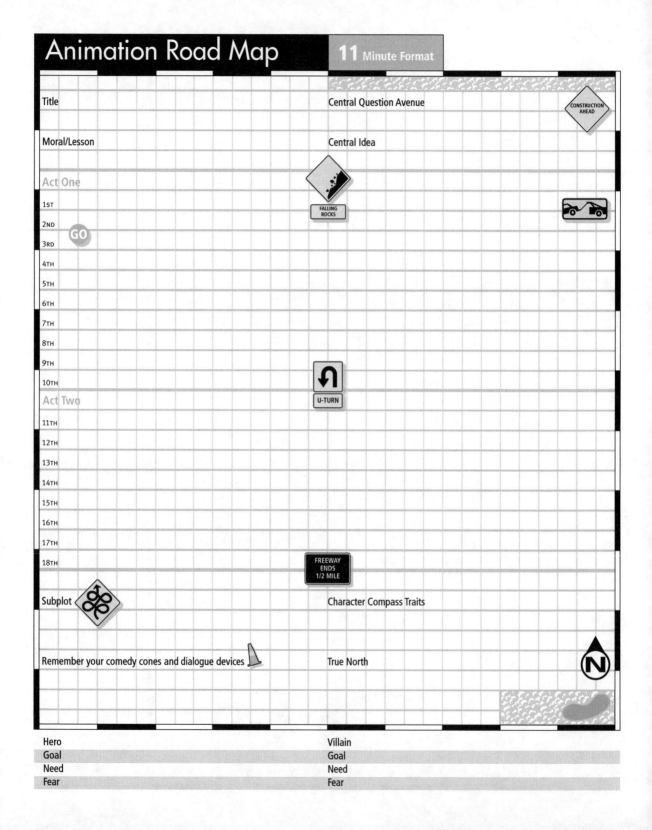

Title

Central Question Avenue

CONSTRUCTION AHEAD

Moral/Lesson

Central Idea

FALLING ROCKS

Act One

1ST

2ND   GO

3RD

4TH

5TH

6TH

7TH

8TH

9TH

10TH

U-TURN

Act Two

11TH

12TH

13TH

14TH

15TH

16TH

17TH

18TH

FREEWAY ENDS 1/2 MILE

Subplot

Character Compass Traits

Remember your comedy cones and dialogue devices

True North

N

Hero	Villain
Goal	Goal
Need	Need
Fear	Fear

Animation Road Map

7 Minute Format

Title

Central Question Avenue

CONSTRUCTION AHEAD

Moral/Lesson

Central Idea

Act One

1ST GO
2ND
3RD
4TH
5TH
6TH
7TH
8TH
9TH
10TH
11TH
12TH
13TH
14TH
15TH

ROAD WIDENS

Subplot

Character Compass Traits

Remember your comedy cones and dialogue devices

True North

N

Hero	Villain
Goal	Goal
Need	Need
Fear	Fear

Appendix

What-A-Mess:
A Birdie in the Paw...

Script by Minda & Marilyn Webber

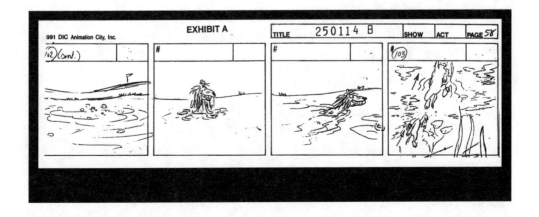

The following 7 minute script was written for the Saturday morning cartoon, *What-A-Mess*. I co-wrote it with my sister and writing partner, Minda Webber. The series is based on a British Children's book series which tells the story of a young pup descended from a champion breed line. What-A-Mess, however, is just that, a complete mess although he dutifully tries hard to live up to his family's reputation. His sidekick, Baldwin, a little bird who nests in the pup's knotted fur, doesn't speak, but provides visual comedy to What-A-Mess's dialogue. Frank is an old English sheep dog and neighbor who speaks with an upper class English accent, while Felicity is the mischievous cat next-door. The parents in the series are like those in *Cow & Chicken*: they are only seen from the waist down or in a way which never reveals their faces, while other adults are shown in complete form. Another fun element to the series, is that throughout the story, gnomes and other animals pop into the scene, sometimes randomly, to add comedic visuals.

A fantasy tunnel, the cartoon series *What-A-Mess* played to the six and under age audience. Notice how the script plays to that audience as you read it. The cartoon series story format varied, using the 11 minute, 7 minute and a three and a half minute episode to fill its 22 minutes on air.

DIC Entertainment, who produced the *What-A-Mess* series generously allowed for the script to be reprinted in this book for which I would like to thank them again. From the 7 minute script, you can get an idea of how screen directions are used and how to format your own animation script.

After reading this script, go back through it and complete the exercises below if you like:

1 List the Tow-Away Street, the Green Light, and the Topper. Next, list the gag sequence.

2 List What-A-Mess's goal.

3 List the comedy cones employed in the script.

"A BIRDIE IN THE PAW…"

FADE IN:

INT. GARAGE - MORNING

What-A-Mess searches through the open garage. Finding the object of his desire, he tears into the bag of fertilizer.

> FRANK (VO)
> In the whole of his long, puppy life, What-A-Mess had heard his mother, The Duchess, say on countless occasions, "that if you do something nice for someone, something nice will happen to you."

What-A-Mess shakes the bag vigorously with teeth, spraying the fertilizer all over the garage.

> FRANK (VO)
> And having heard father say that he needed to get around to spreading that bag of fertilizer in the garage, the young Prince Amir of Kinjan decided to help out, performing his good deed with the most diligent enthusiasm.

> WHAT-A-MESS
> There! Father's sure gonna be surprised.

What-A-Mess surveys the "job" proudly.

> WHAT-A-MESS
> Doing good deeds is kinda fun, huh, Baldwin?

CLOSE ON BALDWIN

Who wears a gas mask and hops on a pogo stick over the fertilizer that's landed in What-A-Mess' fur as he nods vigorously.

BACK TO WHAT-A-MESS

He scans the garage.

> WHAT-A-MESS
> Aha!

WHAT-A-MESS' POV - CLOSE ON WOODEN CLUB

Hanging out of the golf bag that's slid into the backseat, the car door still ajar.

EXT. DRIVEWAY - CONTINUOUS

What-A-Mess trots onto the driveway where the car is parked.

> WHAT-A-MESS
> Boy, I bet doing two good deeds means
> something really, really nice will happen!

CLOSE ON BALDWIN

Who holds a clipboard reading "Good Deeds" with numbers following. He checks off "good deed #2."

BACK TO WHAT-A-MESS

Who gnaws and gnaws until he chews the wooden golf club in half.

> FRANK (VO)
> And so the honorable Prince of Kinjan rushed
> to Father's aid once again, performing, surely, a
> most cherished deed.

> WHAT-A-MESS
> There! Now, that old door will shut.
> (yawning)
> Hmmmm…

What-A-Mess starts to push the door closed when he notices a warm, woolly blanket in the floor board. The sun shines down on it invitingly.

> WHAT-A-MESS
> Maybe I'll just have a little nap before lunch.

INT. CAR - CONTINUOUS

What-A-Mess hops in, and pulls the door shut with his teeth. He snuggles under the blanket in the floorboard for a little nap and SIGHS CONTENTEDLY.

DISSOLVE TO:

EXT. CAR - A SHORT WHILE LATER

The car drives along the rolling landscape.

INT. CAR - CONTINUOUS

CAMERA PANS FROM the sleeping What-A-Mess under the blanket in the back seat to the front seat where Father and Mother, decked out in their sport's sneakers and golf shoes, drive along.

                              MOTHER'S (VO)
                         This is where we're going?

                              FATHER'S (VO)
                         You said you wanted to do something fun and
                         romantic and spontaneous. Well, here we are.

EXT. GOLF COURSE - CONTINUOUS

The car passes under the sign as they enter the golf course.

CLOSE ON SIGN: Which reads "PAR-FECT GOLF COURSE"

(GNOMES bungy jump from the golf sign.)

INT. CAR - CONTINUOUS

Mother's sneaker taps.

                              MOTHER'S (VO)
                         When I said we should spend more time
                         together, golfing wasn't exactly what I had in
                         mind.

Father waves his hand, shrugging -

                              FATHER'S (VO)
                         You'll love it. Trust me.

EXT. CAR - CONTINUOUS

They park, hopping out of the car.

                              MOTHER'S (VO)
                         Alright, but you're carrying the clubs.

Father takes the bag out of the car, not noticing What-A-Mess under the blanket. They
walk off, the golf bag concealing all but their legs and feet.

INT. CAR - CONTINUOUS

The shutting of the door, awakens a sleepy What-A-Mess as Father and Mother head for
the fairway.

                              WHAT-A-MESS
                         (yawning)

The pup crawls out from under the blanket.

> WHAT-A-MESS
> Hey, where are we?!

CLOSE ON BALDWIN

Dressed like an explorer, he has a map in front of him and studies his compass.

EXT. GOLF COURSE - BACK TO WHAT-A-MESS

As he hops out of the car, looking around him. His eyes grow big.

> WHAT-A-MESS
> Wow!

What-A-Mess races across the freshly cut green grass, slipping and sliding across the fairway -

> FRANK (VO)
> As the young prince trotted regally towards the
> lush green lawns…

What-A-Mess rolls around on the fairway, ecstatic.

> FRANK (VO) (CONT.)
> …he realized his Mother was right. Something
> nice did happen in reward for his good deeds.

What-A-Mess comes to a halt, leaping up and looking around, not knowing what to partake of next!

> FRANK (VO) (CONT.)
> There were ponds to splash through …

EXT. WATER TRAP - CONTINUOUS

What-A-Mess leaps into a shallow water trap and splashes through it, emerging on the other side with a lily pad stuck to him.

> FRANK (VO) (CONT.)
> …little white balls flying in the air to chase…

EXT. FAIRWAY - CONTINUOUS

What-A-Mess stops in his soggy tracks as GOLFERS tee off and balls zoom over him right and left.

> WHAT-A-MESS
> Oh, Baldwin - look! There must be a zillion
> balls, or maybe even a hundred!

CLOSE ON BALDWIN

Who wears an accountant's hat and tabulates on an adding machine, the tape winding down onto the golf course.

BACK TO WHAT-A-MESS - COMIC ANGLES

As What-A-Mess leaps into the air snatching balls this way and that way.

FULL ON

GOLFER #1 who is on all fours, lining up his shot on the green. What-A-Mess bounces off his back, using it as a springboard to make another mid-air catch.

> GOLFER #1
>
> Ouuuuufffff!

WIDE ON SCENE

As GOLFER #2 scans the horizon for his ball just as What-A-Mess catches it in his jaws and whisks it away.

> GOLFER #2
>
> (gasps)

Hey, you furry mutt, whaddya think you're doing?!

BACK TO WHAT-A-MESS

Who is oblivious. He stops to rest, his mouth comically full of balls.

CLOSE ON WHAT-A-MESS' EYES

Which bulge with excitement.

> FRANK (VO)
> And most wonderful of all, there was a large
> sandbox in which to bury all his newly acquired
> souvenirs. Yes, the young Prince was in truly in
> puppy heaven.

EXT. SAND TRAP - CONTINUOUS

What-A-Mess digs rapidly, flinging dirt everywhere.

CLOSE ON BALDWIN

Who dodges as a BEETLE in a bulldozer drives past, scooping the sand that's landing in What-A-Mess' fur and lifting it into a dump truck driven by a TICK.

BACK TO WHAT-A-MESS

Who then spits the balls out with machine gun precision into the deep hole.

> WHAT-A-MESS
> Boy, this is the life! Gosh, it's a shame Felicia
> isn't here. She'd sure love this huge kitty box.

(A turtle comes and sits on top of the golf balls as if they were eggs. It takes out some yarn and continues knitting pink and blue booties as it waits for the "eggs" to hatch.)

EXT. FAIRWAY - CONTINUOUS

What-A-Mess suddenly spies Father and Mother across the course.

> WHAT-A-MESS
> Hey, there's my Family! They must have done a
> good deed too.

CLOSE ON BALDWIN

Who is dressed as Santa Claus. He searches through his list of

good deed doers - Can't seem to find them - There they are -

CLOSE ON LIST

Which reads "Father and Mother…Bought new slippers for What-A-Mess to chew."

BACK TO WHAT-A-MESS

In the distance, Mother and Father walk over the hill. What-A-Mess BARKS, but they are too far away to hear him. He frowns and trots across the fairway to catch them.

EXT. ANOTHER PART OF THE FAIRWAY - CONTINUOUS

Father searches through the bag for his beloved club.

> FATHER'S (VO)
> Alright. Now watch how I hold the club, and
> prepare for my swing -

He pulls out the club that What-A-Mess has chewed off -

> FATHER'S (VO)
> What?!

CLOSE ON WOODEN CLUB - IT'S END CHEWED OFF

FATHER'S (VO)

I don't even want to know!

Father sticks the club back into the bag and takes out another club, inspecting it closely this time.

FATHER'S (VO)

(clears his throat)

As I was saying, Rule #1: Always keep your eye on the ball.

Father swings. His ball lands near the flag on the green.

MOTHER'S (VO)

That doesn't look so difficult.

Mother takes the club, pauses, getting her stance just right. Finally, she swings.

DRAMATIC ANGLES

As she hits the ball on her <u>backswing</u>, knocking it in the opposite direction.

FATHER'S (VO)

Oh, my -

The ball hits a golf cart and bounces into a grove of trees, ricocheting through them like in a pin ball machine.

MOTHER'S (VO)

(gleefully)

Oh, you're right, dear. This is fun!

FATHER'S (VO)

(to himself)

I can't watch this.

Her ball whams into the flag pole and is then catapulted back, hitting Father in the rear.

FATHER'S (VO)

Yeow!

MOTHER'S (VO)

Ah, dear? I believe you took your eye off the
ball.

She starts down the fairway as Father rubs his backside and leans over to pick up her ball.

FATHER'S (VO)

(moans to himself)

It's going to be a long day.

EXT. ANOTHER PART OF THE GOLF COURSE - CONTINUOUS

What-A-Mess trots carefree across the green towards them. Then suddenly -

> FRANK'S (VO)
> And as the wily pup searched for his Family, he
> got a most aspiring idea.

What-A-Mess sees a LADY GOLFER WITH PURPLE SOCKS AND BEEHIVE HAIRDO "in need." She takes out a club and walks down the slope to the green. Thinking she's forgotten her bag, What-A-Mess takes the handle in his teeth and hurries down the slope to give the golf bag to her.

> FRANK (VO) (CONT.)
> So many people about, so many good deeds to
> be done.

As the pup drags the bag, the clubs bounce out behind him. The pup trips up in the strap and the now light bag flips up over him, landing on top of his head.

> FRANK (VO) (CONT.)
> Why, he, the Prince thought, might even make
> a Doggie World Record for the most good
> deeds done in a single day. And then, who
> knew what could happen -

COMIC ANGLE AS

A "squeezed-up" What-A-Mess hobbles trying to get the bag off. He bangs into the Lady Golfer with purple socks as she lines up her shot. She flies into a sand trap, her legs flailing about.

> LADY GOLFER
> Ohhh!

What-A-Mess bumps the bag into the Lady Golfer's golf cart and sends it rolling down the slope.

> FRANK (VO) (CONT.)
> - And perhaps he could stay in this delightful
> haven for a whole week.

DRAMATIC ANGLE

As it picks up speed and rams into another cart causing a domino effect with two more carts - Their carts SPLASHES into a water trap!

> GOLFERS
> (ad lib shouts)

(GNOMES play leap frog with real FROGS. Other GNOMES ski past on the pond, their ski ropes attached to DRAGONFLIES.)

The pup crawls out of the bag, unaware of the chaos. What-A-Mess proudly hurries towards Mother and Father as the Angry Golfers wade out of the water trap, lily pads or pond weeds on their heads.

                                                              CUT TO:

EXT. ANOTHER GREEN - CONTINUOUS

A BOWLEGGED, VERY INTENSE GOLFER wearing plaid Bermuda shorts, geometrically lines up his shot on a PAR THREE HOLE.

A small GROUP watches breathlessly. The GOLF DIRECTOR with pristine tacky white golf shoes stands near them.

                         GOLF DIRECTOR
                   Quiet, everyone, Quiet! There's ten thousand
                   dollars riding on this shot! But keep in mind -
                   Not one golfer has made a hole in one on this
                   green in the past twelve years.

                           THE GROUP
                      (ad lib oohs and ahhhs)

Tension mounts as the Very Intense Golfer prepares his shot.

                         GOLF DIRECTOR
                   If he makes it, he'll leave a wealthy man, if
                   not...Shhhh! He's ready to take this challenge.

DRAMATIC ANGLE

As the Golfer swings. The ball bounces, rolling past the sand trap and towards the hole - closer - closer - and -

What-A-Mess whisks INTO FRAME, snatching the ball from the hole, saving it just in time!

                         WHAT-A-MESS
                   Whew! That was close. This one almost got
                   lost in that ole hole.

Clueless, What-A-Mess continues on to find his Family.

                           FRANK (VO)
                   And so content with the fact that surely he had
                   set a new Doggie World Record, and still
                   unaware of the mounting attention his good

deeds were cultivating, the admirable Prince of
Kinjan decided to find his Family.

EXT. GREEN - CONTINUOUS

The Very Intense Golfer hits the ground, kicking and screaming -

> INTENSE GOLFER
> (crying)
> He took my ball! Did you see that? It's not fair!
> You're all witnesses! What is that, that, that -
> that <u>dog</u> doing on the course?!

Golfer #1, Lady Golfer, and the rest of the water trap Mob catch up to them.

> GOLFER #1
> Yeah, and that furball buried my ball!

> LADY GOLFER
> That's nothing! He ruined my new hairdo! I
> spent hours at the beauty parlor and look at it!

CLOSE ON HER BEEHIVE

Which is now a flat top with sticks and sand crabs.

BACK TO SCENE

Fists wave in the air -

> OTHER GOLFERS
> (join in ad lib complaints)

> GOLF DIRECTOR
> I don't what's going on here, but I give you the
> word of Silas P. Boggerty that I'll get to the
> bottom of this outrage at once!

The Golf Director leads the mob as they trail after the oblivious What-A-Mess.

CUT TO:

EXT. ANOTHER PART OF THE GOLF COURSE - CONTINUOUS

Father reaches to take out his favorite club and is about to swing when he realizes it's the
chewed club.

> FATHER'S (VO)
> Agghhh! That's it!

He breaks it in two and picks out another club.

                    MOTHER'S (VO)
          Now, dear, we're suppose to be having fun.

What-A-Mess comes upon Mother and Father on the green.

                    FATHER'S (VO)
          …Okay, how about livening things up with a
          little wager? Whoever gets their ball in the hole
          first, wins the whole game. If I win, you have to
          cook me a steak dinner on the grill. And if you
          win, you get to pick the night's entertainment -
          Anything you want.

                    MOTHER'S (VO)
          Anything?

                    FATHER'S (VO)That's right. Anything.

                    MOTHER'S (VO)
          It's a deal.

He prepares to swing.

                    FATHER'S (VO)
          Good. Oh, and remember, I like my T-Bone,
          medium rare.

                    MOTHER'S (VO)
          Don't be so cocky. It's not over until the fat
          lady sings.

(CHUBBY OPERA FEMALE GNOME in Viking costume sings dramatically and the
GNOME AUDIENCE applauds from the opera balcony inside the gold hole.)

Father laughs as he swings.

                    FRANK (VO)
          You'll have to make a hole in one. I can't wait
          to see that!

                                                            CUT TO:

What-A-Mess who comes up behind them.

                    WHAT-A-MESS
          Hey, they want the ball in the hole! This should
          be a cinch!

Mother swings, but puts a little too much swing in her swing. They can't see where their balls have landed, but as they watch Mother's ball descend over the hill, they hear a SPLASH.

> FATHER'S (VO)
> I can taste that steak right now.

They walk up the hill.

EXT. GREEN AND WATER TRAP - CONTINUOUS

What-A-Mess dives into the water trap after Mother's ball. He scoops it up from just below the surface and dog paddles towards shore. Underneath his legs -

(Underwater is a "graveyard" of golf balls with little tomb- stones. A funeral carriage drawn by a crawfish and driven by a lost watch, its hands holding the reigns, cart off another golf ball to the underwater cemetery.)

What-A-Mess leaps from the pond and hurries to drop the ball into the hole as Father and Mother come over the hill and onto the green.

> FATHER'S (VO)
> What-A-Mess?!

> MOTHER'S (VO)
> Where'd you come from?

What-A-Mess BARKS proudly at Mother's soggy ball in the hole; Father's is several feet away.

> MOTHER'S (VO)
> I guess this means you'll be escorting me to the ballet.

> FATHER'S (VO)
> The ballet?!

Mother hugs What-A-Mess.

> MOTHER'S (VO)
> (whispering to the pup)
> But I think someone here does deserve a steak dinner for his good deed.

What-A-Mess is happy to hear that!

> FRANK (VO)
> The joyous moment ended abruptly, however, as the rest of Prince Amir's grateful fans came to pay their parting farewells.

An army of GOLF CLEATS charge towards them, the Golf Director and Very Intense Golfer leading the mob.

MOB
(ad lib mumblings)

LADY GOLFER

There he is!

GOLF DIRECTOR
Never in the history of Par-Fect Golf Course
has there ever been such a day!

What-A-Mess smiles proudly - he must have made a record! What-A-Mess shakes the pond water off onto the mob, spraying them.

MOB

Ahhhhhh!

FATHER'S (VO)
I guess that's a game. Let's go!

Mother and Father chuckle as they hurry off.

MOTHER'S (VO)
You were right dear. Golfing is fun.

EXT. FAMILY BACKYARD - THAT NIGHT

Mother cooks a SIZZLING steak. She takes it off the grill and puts it on a plate as Father walks in dressed in his tuxedo.

FATHER'S (VO)
(grumbling)
Medium rare. That's just how I like it.

Mother hands the steak to What-A-Mess who licks his lips.

MOTHER'S (VO)
Ready for the ballet, Dear?

FRANK (VO)
(sighing)

Yes.

As they walk out, What-A-Mess chows down on his delicious reward.

THE END

Index